SEX DIFFERENCES AROUND THE WORLD IN TIME DISTANCE WATCH

Life Expectancy, Obesity, Mean Body Mass Index, and Diabetes for about 200 Countries

PAVLE SICHERL

Gaptimer Report No. 5

Copyright © 2016 Pavle Sicherl

Ljubljana, June 2016

Layout and Figures: Jaka Hajnšek

Printed by CreateSpace, An Amazon.com Company.

ISBN 978-1534708389

FOREWORD

The book offers new insights by examining gender differences in life expectancy, mean body mass index, obesity and diabetes by using the novel time distance methodology. The art of handling different views of data is crucial for discovering the relevant patterns and for providing a broader framework for policy and business analysis. The gender difference in these indicators can be appealing from both the medical and social standpoint and these results can be further elaborated in much more details with additional studies.

Sustainable development is by definition a long-run and multi-dimensional phenomenon. Semantics of discussing the issues, in setting the targets and in the implementation should not be based only on static measures; it needs to be complemented by dynamic measures. This methodology presents an innovation that goes beyond the present state-of-the art in measuring the degree of inequality increasing the understanding of the situation in the time perspective.

The study of gender differences over long period of time was possible for life expectancy with UN data for quite some time but the extension to body mass index and diabetes was made available by two studies in Lancet: the study of trends in adult body-mass index (NCD Risk Factor Collaboration; NCD-RisC, 2016a) and the study on diabetes (NCD-RisC, 2016b) (and with more details on www.ncdrisc.org). They present a very remarkable broad effort for preparing the database and analysis on these topics. The well documented disaggregated data are accompanied with nice visualization tools thus allowing the study of a number of points of interest. Here we shall concentrate on gender difference within countries in these indicators which can be of interest from both the medical and social standpoint for further studies. The availability of 200 country data over the four decades makes it possible to describe the magnitude of gender disparities in two dimensions: static and time distance.

Time distance methodology can be very helpful both on the aggregate and national levels. It is a generic methodology, applicable to many domains beyond gender disparity and many indicators beyond the selected indicators here. Potential users of this methodology could be international and national organizations, NGOs, experts, businesses, managers, educators, students, interest groups, media, and general public at the world, national, and lower levels.
This analysis of gender inequality in selected fields deals mostly with the first part of the statement of Aristotel, "Let us first understand the facts, and then we may seek the cause". Namely, the multiple factors behind the astonishing magnitude of country differences in the gender gap in life expectancy are very complex and interconnected; they include medical, social, and economic factors requiring large systematic research project(s).

Ljubljana, June 2016   Pavle Sicherl

TABLE OF CONTENTS

Chapter 1

INTRODUCTION

Describing and perceiving inequalities in terms of percentages and ranks is not the end of the story. Development processes take place in time, and time is important as an operational and comparative metric.

The statistical picture of disparities is presented by using three descriptive measures (absolute and relative static measures as well as S-time-distance measure as a special family of time distance measures defined for the level of the indicator). Expressed in time units, the time distance approach is easy to understand and provides a useful complement to existing methods providing new insights from existing data.

This study also contributes some novel methodological tools that can be usefully applied for other indicators in analysing gender and other disparities, both at macro and micro levels. Namely, measurement is costly and it is important how efficiently we exploit existing data for building knowledge and for policy debate. The statistical results are raising questions for further analysis of the reasons that the gender disparity in life expectancy is so much in favour of women around the globe in contrast to so many fields of concern where the gender disparity is in many countries very much tilted in the other direction.

Chapter 2 will serve two purposes. On the one hand it will concentrate on gender disparity in life expectancy at various levels (at the world level for 200 countries and some aggregates; for EU countries, and draws also some conclusions at the regional level of NUTS1 and NUTS2 for EU and also from the study of more than 3000 USA counties). On the other hand, life expectancy will serve as the indicator for the example how the time distance methodology can convey additional insights and understanding from the available data.

The study looks at two major points: that female life expectancy at birth is higher than that for males for 99.5 percent of the world population, on the one hand and that there is an astonishing great dispersion of this gender difference among countries, on the other. Two major statistical sources used are The UN World Population Prospects (The 2015 Revision) for the period 1950–2015 (UN, 2015), NCD-RisC (2016c), and Eurostat databases for some comparisons.

At the theoretical level the time distance methodology adds innovative dual parallel generic system for analyzing indicators in the parallel universe of time beyond the static differences, adding new vocabulary and is not replacing the current methods. Empirically, the degree of disparity may be very different in static terms and in time distance, which leads to new conclusions and semantics important for policy considerations. The approach is universal, expressed in time units it is easily understandable by everyone, and applicable to a wide variety of fields at both the macro and micro levels. Since time distance view provides an additional dimension of temporal disparity, results by other methods are left unchanged but new conclusions can be reached.

Chapter 3 deals with gender disparities in EU28 countries. On the one hand the methodological topics of time matrices, and the calculations of S-time-distances and S-time-steps for these countries are presented also in the novel visualisation format. The important conclusion indicates that the gender differences in life expectancy are very large also between EU countries and not only in the whole world as shown in Chapter 2.

In Chapter 4 the earlier discussion of gender differences in life expectancy at birth is here continued for three indicators: mean body mass index, obesity and diabetes. S-time-distances show large time lags between the genders for mean BMI, for 20 countries in favour of men and for 45 countries in favour for women (when the time distances are larger than 20 years in either direction). Longer time series of data allowed us to describe how the mean BMI gender differences prevailed over longer periods of time, in one set of countries with male BMI ahead of the female, in a larger set of countries in the other direction.

Obesity differences are much more tilted as dominant on the female side, there are no countries where male time lead would exceed 20 years. Diabetes is another story, here male lead in time distance over 20 years is seen in 34 countries as against the female lead of that magnitude only in 3 countries.

Chapter 5 summarises the time distance distribution of countries by male female lead or lag for the four selected indicators. It recapitulates the situation that two of them, life expectancy and obesity, contain only country cases where women would be ahead of men for more than 20 years. The situation is strongly asymmetrical for longer stability of the gender difference in this direction. Mean BMI is already more balanced, with diabetes showing male predominance but not of the same strong view of dominance as it was indicated for women in the first three analysed fields.

Chapter 2

GENDER DIFFERENCES IN LIFE EXPECTANCY IN THE TIME DISTANCE PERSPECTIVE

Methodology: Time distance measure as additional perspective in measuring inequalities

Time distance is an innovative approach for looking at time-series data The existing descriptive statistical measures describing disparities are predominantly static. The present state-of-the-art does not realise that, in addition to static comparison, there exists in principle a theoretically equally universal measure of difference (distance) in time when a given level of the variable is attained by the two compared time series.

A brief definition of two novel statistical measures: S-time-distance and S-time-step

The statistical measure S-time-distance measures the distance (proximity) in time between the points in time when the two series compared reach a specified level of the indicator X. For instance, Figure 1 shows that the EU28 life expectancy of 78.1 years was attained by males in 2015 and by females in 1989, S-time-distance amounts to 26 years (2015 minus 1989). This means that at the level of 78.1 years the male life expectancy was lagging in time for 26 years or that the female life expectancy was leading by 26 years. **S-time-distance** for a given level of X_L is defined as:

$$S_{ij} (X_L) = \Delta t (X_L) = t_i (X_L) - t_j (X_L) \qquad (1)$$

The **S-time-step** measures the time elapsed between two levels of a time-series, providing an alternative description of its growth rate, measuring the growth of a series by using the inverse relation to the conventional $\Delta X / \Delta t$ growth rate metrics. For instance, as shown in Figure 8 that EU28 female life expectancy needed in the past about 5.5 years to increase the life expectancy from 82 years to 83 years. This is a complementary description of the dynamics of life expectancy to the conventional growth rate matrix, which would described the dynamics as about 0.3 percentage per year. Both measures are valid description of the dynamics of change, while for general public S-time-step might be even easier to understand. S-time-step is expressed in units of time and is defined as:

$$S_i (\Delta X_L) = [t_i (X_L + \Delta X) - t_i (X_L)] / \Delta X \qquad (2)$$

Further information on the time distance methodology and applications are available in numerous earlier publications like Kyklos (Sicherl, 1973), IB Revija (Sicherl, 1999), Social Indicators Research (Sicherl, 2007), in the paper published by OECD Statistics Directorate (Sicherl, 2011), and most extensively in the book 'Time Distance in Economics and Statistics' (Sicherl, 2012).

Static measures of disparity require no further explanation. Time distance methodology is well positioned to complement them as one of the appropriate tools for the task of measuring disparity. It provides two novel generic descriptive statistical measures to measure the time dimension of these disparities. The time distance approach brings about two persuasive advantages for extensive practical use. Expressed in time units it is intuitively understood by policymakers, professionals, managers, media, and the general public thus facilitating their subjective perception about their position in the society and in the world in this additional dimension. Another technical and presentation advantage is that time and time distance is comparable across variables, fields of concern, and units of comparison. This makes it an excellent analytical, presentation, and communication tool.

Gender inequality in life expectancy – static distance and time distance

Time series can be compared in two dimensions. In Figure 1 we take the example of the gender disparities in life expectancy at birth for EU28 aggregates. One way is to compare time series at the given point in time, i.e. in our case the static gap in life expectancy between women and men in 2015. The absolute difference amounts to 5.3 years; the index is 106.8. Another dimension of the degree of disparity is taking into consideration the distance in years when men and women reached the same reference level of the variable, in our case the life expectancy for men in 2015 was reached by women already in 1989: S-time-distance amounted to 26 years.

Figure 1 illustrates these two dimensions of gender disparities in life expectancy. It shows that perceptions of the size of this gap can be very different depending on the statistical measure used. Here the static difference between two lines in 2015 is less than 7 percent (which may appear to be small) while the time-distance is 26 years (which gives a very different perception of the magnitude of the gap). For realistic evaluation of the situation we need both measures.

The perception of wellbeing and of the degree of disparity is subjective. As shown empirically the degree of disparity may be very different in static terms and in time distance, which leads to new conclusions and semantics important for policy considerations. Different people will give different subjective weights to the static and time distance dimension of disparity and they might be also very different for different indicators. Further discussion on inter-temporal aspect of wellbeing is available in Sicherl (2014a). Different people will give different subjective weights to the static and time distance dimension of disparity and they might be also very different for different indicators.

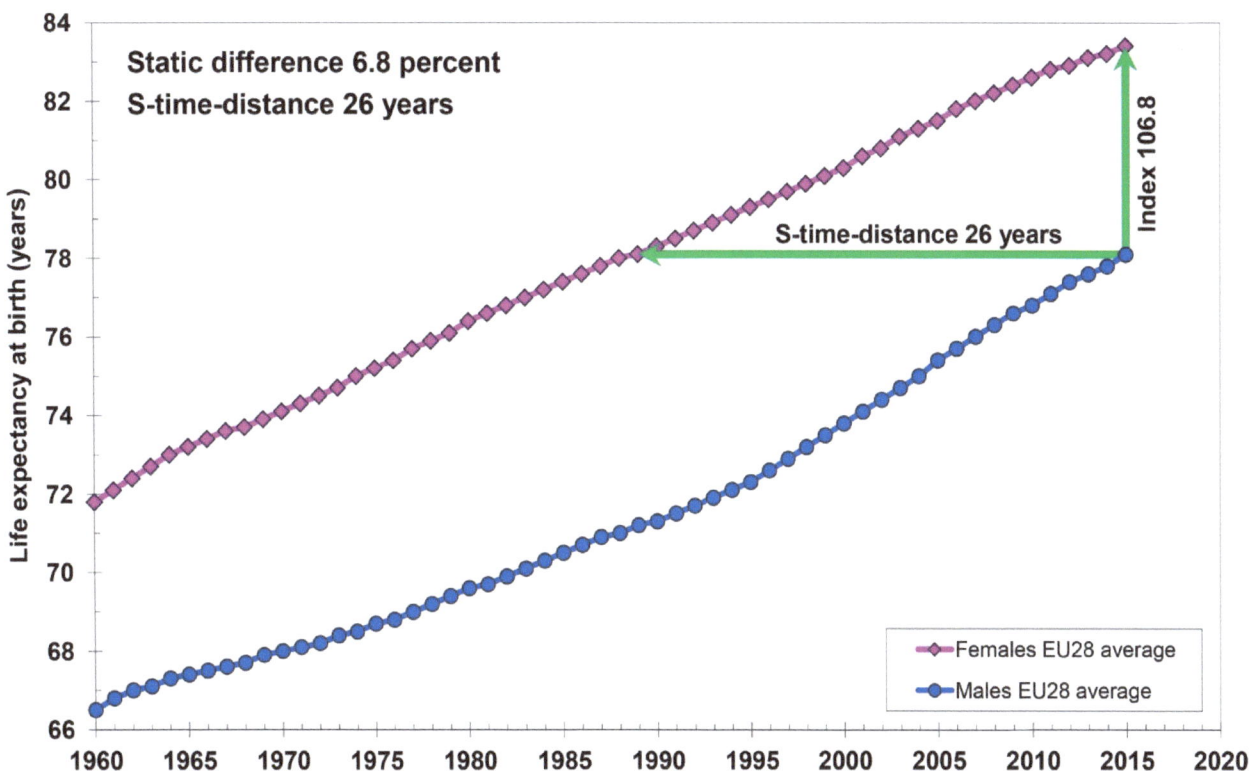

FIGURE 1 Gender disparities in life expectancy at birth, EU28 average in 2015: static index and time distance

SOURCE: Own calculations based on UN (2015).

Table 1 explains the correspondence between the conventional table-format for time-series data, and the complementary presentation based on the time distance approach. It refers to three types of comparisons: the level of the indicators, their dynamics, and comparisons of levels relative to a benchmark.

This schematic presentation shows the correspondence between conventional table format as the starting point in the database and possible additional complementary presentation by time distance approach. The intention is to complement rather than replace the existing mostly static measures to provide a broader dynamic analytical framework.

One of these methodological possibilities is time matrix visualisation over many units and over time. Thus the first complementary presentation refers to the initial data for indicators. For presentation of levels the conventional table-format for time-series data is transformed into time matrix, which has a table-graph format. The identifiers in level-time matrix are units and selected levels of indicator while the corresponding times when these levels were achieved are in the main body of the table, thus turning around the usual X-Y arrangement of axes. Calculating these times by interpolations may pose a small problem of the degree of accuracy compared to original data but it gains additional understanding about time dimension of disparities and a good summary overview.

PRESENTATION OVER MANY UNITS AND OVER TIME
(LONG-TERM)

A. Conventional table format as the base	B. Possible additional complementary presentation

1. DATA FOR INDICATORS (example: life expectancy)

Table

A1	Time			
	1960	...	...	...	**2011**
Countries (units)	Indicator values at specific point in time			

Level-time matrix or table-graph

B1	Indicator value			
	66	...	...	...	**85**
Countries (units)	Time when the selected indicator value was achieved			

2. DYNAMICS AND COMPARISON OF DYNAMICS

Table of growth rates or indices of dynamics

A2	Time			
	1961	...	...	...	**2011**
Countries (units)	Annual growth rate or index of dynamics			

S-time-step (in years)

B2	Indicator value			
	67	...	...	...	**85**
Countries (units)	Time needed to achieve next level of the selected indicator value			

3. COMPARISON OF LEVELS

Index: benchmark = 100 by years

A3	Time			
	1960	...	...	...	**2011**
Countries (units)	Index values by years			

S-time-distance (in years) from benchmark

B3	Indicator value			
	66	...	...	...	**85**
Countries (units)	S-time-distance (in years): - time lead, + time lag from benchmark			

TABLE 1 Schematic presentation of correspondence between conventional table format and additional complementary presentation in time distance approach
Source: Sicherl (2011 and 2012).

In the time matrix data the visual emphasis is on level of indicators. i.e. data are arranged by selected levels of indicators and showing in which year these levels of the indicators were achieved by given country. This format of level-time matrix is easily understood by everybody, at the same time it provides also a simple visualisation tool for many units over time.

Time matrix allows for a quick level comparison:

- of the situation across the selected countries
- of how many steps over levels of indicators a given country has progressed, which is an additional indication of the dynamics in the country.

The use of time-matrix presentation is meant to be complementary to the usual time-series data tables. One of the useful characteristics is that time matrix condenses such information in much smaller number of entries, which is of great advantage for presentation over many units and over time. By itself (i.e. even without calculating the two statistical measures S-time-distance and S-time-step) such matrices can be used in publications, web pages, etc. as a first-level visualisation tool to 'turn statistics into knowledge' (Sicherl, 2011: 30).

The first comparison can start with time matrix visualisation of the selected indicator over many units and over time. There are several examples of time matrices in the report. Figure 2 shows time matrix for female and male life expectancy for the world level and selected world regions (including S-time-distances between them for a given level of the life expectancy). Figure 9 for EU28 shows a combined large time matrix for all EU countries for both genders.

The second complementary presentation refers to dynamics and comparison of dynamics. Table of growth rates or indices of dynamics are complemented with table of S-time-step in Figure 8, which represent time needed to achieve the next level of the selected indicator value.

The third complementary presentation refers to comparison of levels. The index values by years (benchmark=100) is complemented in by the S-time-distance measure in years from the benchmark (– time lead, + time lag from benchmark). S-time-distances for selected levels of X_L are arrived at by subtracting the respective times for a given unit and the times for the benchmark unit. Time distance perspectives of gender inequalities are the focus of analysis in the book.

There are several methods for calculating S-time-distances and S-time-step. One interesting approximate method is calculation of these two statistical measures from the respective time matrices. We can derive two statistical measures, expressed in standardized units of time (S-time-distance and S-time-step) by subtracting the respective times in the series between the compared units for a given level of the indicator or for each unit in the time matrix for consecutive levels of the variable, respectively. For instance, from time matrix in Figure 2 at the level of 68 years of life expectancy, this level for world aggregate was achieved by females around 1998 and males around 2012, subtracting these two times we get a rounded value of S-time-distance of about 14 years. For females the time needed in the past to increase one level of life expectancy 3.5 years were needed to increase life expectancy from 72 years to 73 years, and 3.3 years for males to increase life expectancy from 67 to 68 years. S-time-step as a measure of dynamics for EU28 countries is shown in Figure 8.

Time distances of gender inequalities in life expectancy at the global level

Figure 2 from the UN database (UN 2015) for 200 countries presents an example how the time matrix ft visualisation can at a glance provide comparisons across gender within a group as well as comparisons of levels of either female or male life expectancy among different units shown in the figure.

From the values in the time matrix it is possible to calculate S-time-distances for gender disparity (male to female lag they are presented in the third column for each group). The highest value of life expectancy achieved by both females and males in the world was 68 years. That level was achieved by females in 1998, by males in 2012, so that the S-time-distance amounted to 14 years. The gender time gap for Western Europe was 26 years (at level 79), for Northern America 37 (at level of 77), for Latin America and the Caribbean 21 years (at level 71), for China 11 years (at level 74) and for Africa 5 years (at level 59).

However, in addition to that, one can also observe the time distances between units, not only between males and females for a given unit. For instance, one can calculate from the time matrix the time lead or time lag from benchmark China. China was selected as the benchmark as it has shown the highest increases in life expectancy at birth in Figure 2. The level of 77 years for female life expectancy was attained in China in 2012, in Latin America and the Caribbean in 2008, in Northern America in 1977 and in Western Europe in 1980, and in Australia/New Zealand in 1978. Thus the time distance lag for China at that level of female life expectancy amounted to about 4 years behind Latin America and the Caribbean, and between 32 and 35 years behind Western Europe, Northern America, and Australia/New Zealand.

Level of life expectancy at birth (years)	WORLD Females	WORLD Males	WORLD S-time-distance	Australia/New Zealand Females	Australia/New Zealand Males	Australia/New Zealand S-time-distance	Western Europe Females	Western Europe Males	Western Europe S-time-distance	Northern America Females	Northern America Males	Northern America S-time-distance	Latin America and the Caribbean Females	Latin America and the Caribbean Males	Latin America and the Caribbean S-time-distance	China Females	China Males	China S-time-distance	Africa Females	Africa Males	Africa S-time-distance
84				2012			2015														
83				2005			2008														
82				2001			2003														
81				1996			1998			2009											
80				1991	2013	22	1993			2003											
79				1987	2008	21	1988	2015	26	1991											
78				1981	2004	23	1984	2010	26	1982			2013								
77				1978	2001	23	1980	2006	26	1977	2014	37	2008			2012					
76				1975	1998	23	1976	2003	27	1974	2009	34	2004			2007					
75				1972	1995	24	1972	2000	28	1971	2004	32	2001			2004					
74				1960	1992	32	1966	1997	31	1966	1999	34	1998			2002	2013	11			
73	2014			1955	1988	33	1961	1993	32	1958	1995	38	1995			1999	2008	9			
72	2010			1952	1985	33	1958	1988	31	1954	1991	37	1993			1996	2004	9			
71	2007				1981		1955	1984	29	1950	1984	34	1990	2012	21	1992	2002	10			
70	2005				1978		1952	1980	28		1979		1988	2007	20	1986	2000	14			
69	2002				1975			1976			1976		1985	2003	19	1982	1998	15			
68	1998	2012	14		1970			1969			1973		1982	2000	18	1980	1995	15			
67	1993	2008	15		1953			1960			1969		1980	1997	17	1978	1987	9			
66	1988	2006	17					1955			1954		1978	1995	17	1976	1983	6			
65	1985	2003	18					1952					1975	1992	17	1975	1980	5			
64	1982	2000	18										1973	1989	17	1974	1978	4			
63	1979	1996	17										1971	1986	15	1972	1976	4			
62	1977	1991	14										1969	1983	14	1971	1975	3	2015		
61	1975	1986	12										1967	1980	13	1970	1974	3	2013		
60	1972	1983	11										1965	1977	12	1970	1973	3	2011		
59	1970	1980	10										1963	1974	11	1969	1972	3	2009	2015	5
58	1969	1977	8										1961	1971	10	1968	1971	2	2008	2012	4
57	1967	1975	7										1959	1968	9	1968	1970	2	2007	2010	3
56	1966	1972	6										1958	1966	8	1967	1969	2	2005	2009	3
55	1965	1970	5										1956	1963	7	1967	1969	2	2004	2007	3
54	1964	1968	5										1954	1961	7	1966	1968	2	2001	2006	5
53	1963	1967	5										1953	1959	6	1966	1968	2	1986	2004	19
52	1961	1966	5										1951	1957	6	1966	1967	2	1982	2002	20
51	1958	1965	6											1955		1965	1967	2	1980	1999	19
50	1956	1963	8											1953		1965	1966	2	1977	1987	9
49	1954	1961	8											1952		1964	1966	2	1975	1983	8
48	1952	1959	7													1964	1965	2	1973	1980	7
47	1950	1956	6													1963	1965	2	1971	1977	7
46		1954														1962	1964	2	1968	1975	7
45		1952														1961	1964	3	1966	1973	7
44																1951	1963	12	1964	1970	7
43																	1962		1961	1968	6
42																	1960		1959	1965	6
41																			1957	1963	6
40																			1955	1960	5
39																			1953	1958	5
38																			1952	1956	5
37																				1954	
36																				1952	

Legend: Females   Males   S-time-distance (in years): Time lag of males behind females

FIGURE 2 Time matrix for selected units: female life expectancy, male life expectancy, S-time-distances between them for a given level of the life expectancy
SOURCE: Own calculations based on UN (2015).

For males the time distances of China behind the more advanced regions are smaller than of females. At the level of male life expectancy at 74 years, China arrived at that level in 2013, Northern America in 1999, Western Europe in 1997, and Australia/New Zealand in 1992. At that level male life expectancy was lagging behind Northern America for 14 years, behind Western Europe for 16 years, and behind Australia/New Zealand 21 years, For male life expectancy at birth China was, however, 10 years ahead Latin America and Caribbean (level 71), 17 ahead of world average (level 68), and 43 years ahead of Africa (level 59); Latin

America and Caribbean and Africa were behind China.

It is interesting to observe the changing position of China during the analysed period. In the late-1960s, at level of life expectancy for females of 58 years and of male value of 54 years, China crossed from the position of being below the world level to the being above that, increasing their lead against the world level to 15 years for women (level 73) and for 17 years for men (level 68). The three advanced units in the table were always ahead, and Africa behind China.

Vertical comparisons show also at a glance the range of values achieved for a given unit over the period of available data. In absolute terms obviously the greatest increase was achieved in China, for both female and male life expectancy. It is remarkable that during 1960s the life expectancy was growing so fast that an increase of life expectancy of 1 year was achieved on the average of about each 8 months period. Even Africa increased life expectancy for more years than the three most advanced units in the table, both in absolute and in relative terms, which confirms that at the higher levels life expectancy is more difficult to increase.

S-time-step as an example of measure of dynamics as calculated from values in Figure 2, is showing the number of years needed to achieve the next level of the indicator, can be easily calculated by subtracting the years in each column for female or male life expectancy (e.g., for females to increase life expectancy at the world level from 71 to 72 years 2.7 years were needed and for males to increase from 66 to 67 years 2.8 years were needed. At the highest level Australia/New Zealand needed about 6.5 years to increase the female life expectancy from 83 to 84 years, and for male life expectancy 5 years were needed for increase from 79 to 80 years).

Trends in the world we are analysing according to the UN classification to take advantage of their data; in this source MDR comprise Europe, Northern America, Australia/New Zealand, and Japan.

In 2015 the range of absolute difference in life expectancy at birth between females and males ranges from 3.8 years for least developed countries to 6.2 years for more developed regions. Data for aggregates indicate a conclusion that the female-male disparity at life expectancy at birth is higher in more developed than in the less developed region. This conclusion might be rather different at country or regional level in some parts of the world. Without major changes in health conditions the UN estimates expect that the higher female than male life expectancy at birth is to be a condition to prevail over the period of 150 years.

The conclusion that the female life expectancy is higher than that for males is confirmed also at the country level for 97% of 196 countries in the UN 2010 Revision. The countries with that exception vary. Only in the period 1950–1980 estimates show that Southern Asia (Afghanistan, Bangladesh, India, Iran, Maldives, and Nepal) experienced the situation that the life expectancy was higher for men than for women. In the period 2005–2010 this was true for only six countries, mostly in Africa (Zimbabwe, Lesotho, Botswana, Swaziland, Malawi, and Qatar; only a very small share of 0.5% of the world population). Life expectancy at birth is at present higher for females than for males in 99.5% of the world population. For 2015 only in two countries, Swaziland and Mali, life expectancy for men were higher than for women.

Time	World	MDR	USA	EU28	LDR	China	India
1960	3.2	5.9	6.5	5.3	2.1	2.8	-1.5
1965	3.6	6.4	7.1	5.8	2.2	3.3	-1.4
1970	3.9	6.9	7.6	6.1	2.5	3.6	-1.1
1975	4	7.3	7.7	6.5	2.6	2.8	-0.5
1980	4.4	7.6	7.5	6.8	3	2.9	0.2
1985	4.4	7.3	7.2	6.9	3.2	3.2	0.3
1990	4.5	7.4	7	7	3.3	3.3	0.7
1995	4.7	7.7	6.4	7	3.4	3.7	1.3
2000	4.4	7.5	5.5	6.5	3.4	3.4	1.7
2005	4.3	7.3	5.1	6.1	3.3	3	1.7
2010	4.5	6.7	4.9	5.8	3.6	3.1	2.3
2015	4.5	6.2	4.7	5.3	3.8	3	3

TABLE 2 Gender disparities in life expectancy in years (Female minus Male)
SOURCE: Based on data from UN (2015).

Time	World	MDR	USA	EU28	LDR	China	India
1960	7.5	9.8			5.2		-2.3
1965	5.7	13.1		14.7	2.3	1.8	-2.0
1970	5.1	17.5		18.3	2.8	2.2	-1.6
1975	7.4	21.7		22.0	4.5	3.4	-0.7
1980	9.6	25.7		25.2	5.8	4.9	0.3
1985	11.2	28.8	35.0	28.3	7.4	7.7	1.0
1990	13.5	32.8	37.7	31.3	9.3	11.2	1.4
1995	16.8	37.4	38.5	33.3	11.8	14.8	2.3
2000	18.0	40.8	33.5	31.5	12.7	13.5	3.6
2005	17.5	42.3	33.3	29.0	11.0	8.3	4.5
2010	14.5	38.5	35.3	28.0	10.0	10.0	5.0
2015	13.7	37.5	37.7	26.0	10.8	12.3	6.8

TABLE 3 S-time-distance (in years): Time lag for males behind females life expectancy for a given level of males
SOURCE: Own calculations based on data from UN (2015).

As we have seen in the example for the EU28 average in Figure 1 the time distance dimension of the gender disparity was very high. For the world average in 2015 in Table 3 the S-time-distance was 13.7 years, which means that the level of male life expectancy in 2015 was attained by females already around 2001. For the more developed regions S-time-distance amounted to 37.5 years and for the less developed regions to 10.8 years.

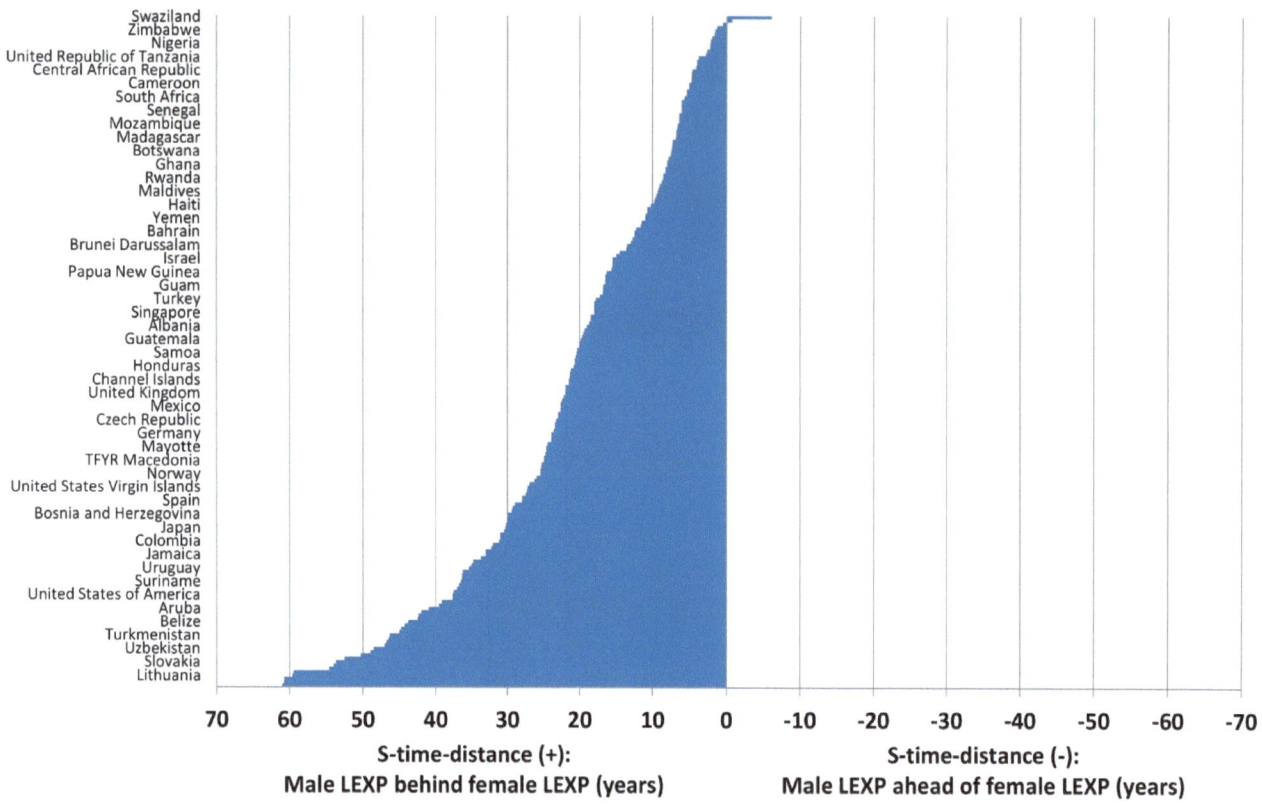

FIGURE 3 Time distance between male and female life expectancy at birth in 2015

SOURCE: Own calculations based on data from UN (2015).

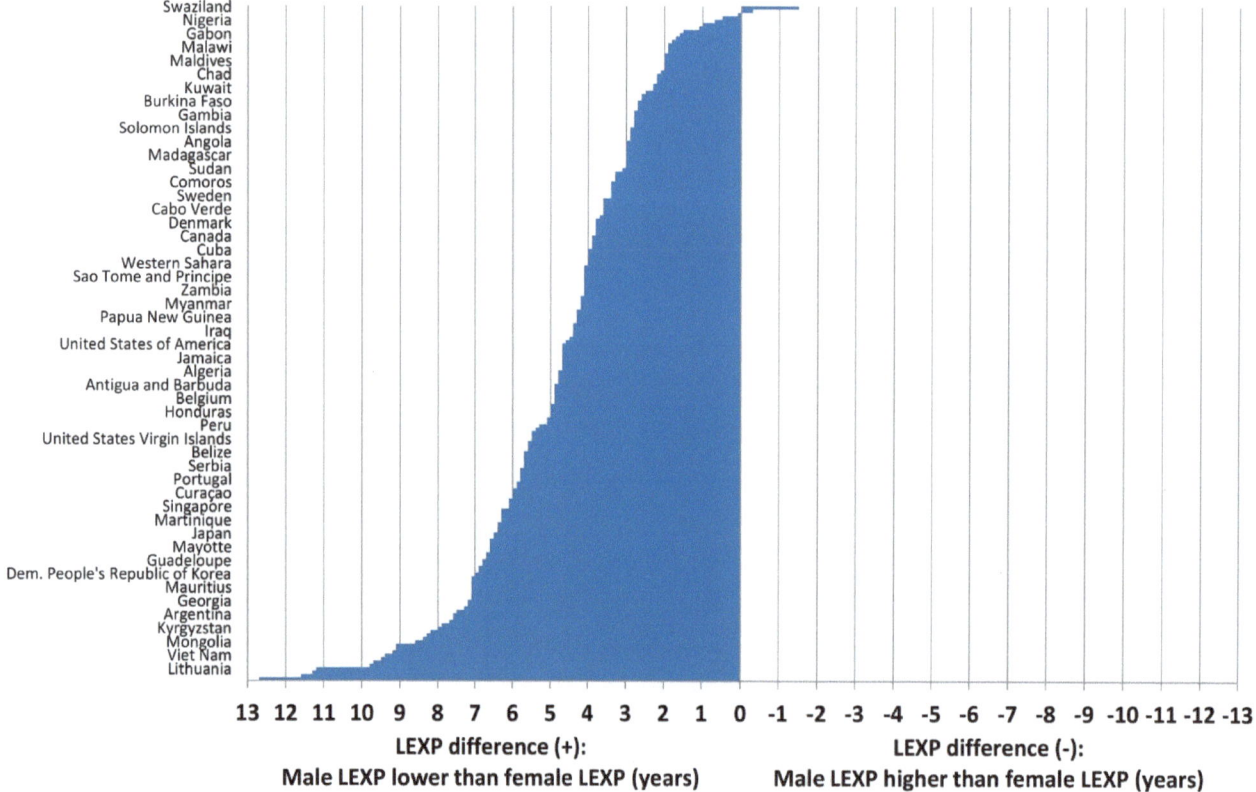

FIGURE 4 Absolute difference between female and male life expectancy at birth in 2015

NOTES: Because of the high number of countries included, on the vertical axis only every fourth country name is shown.

SOURCE: Own calculations based on data from UN (2015).

The time distance lag of male levels behind the same levels of female life expectancy can be further illustrated in Figure 3 over the whole range of 200 countries from the UN (2015) database. For each of these countries it was calculated how many years earlier were the 2015 values of male life expectancy attained by female life expectancy in the same country The median S-time-distance amounted to 20 years, for 101 countries the time lag was even higher than that. For 5 countries it was higher than 55 years, for three even more than 60 years. Though the S-time-distances for the past should not be taken as prediction for the future these values indicate that the gender disparity in life expectancy is very persistent and will be in most countries very difficult to eliminate.

Wide gender differences around the world

Figure 5 shows that female-male difference in life expectancy was much higher in the aggregate for more developed regions than in the aggregate for less developed regions. However, this does not mean that higher income level should be considered as a single most important factor for the female-male difference. The factors contributing to gender differences in life expectancy are much more complicated.

On the more detailed disaggregation of world regions the ranks are shown by the magnitude of the gender disparity in life expectancy. By far the highest female-male differences are shown for Eastern Europe and Central Asia; for the former the difference amounts to nearly 10 years and for the latter for nearly 8 years, while the world average is more than 4 years. Both of these regions were a part of the political system prevailing in the former Soviet Union and in the associated countries. So for Eastern Europe one of the factors may be the position of women in the society over a long period, the history as well as the life style of men as the ranking of the male life expectancy in countries of Eastern Europe is much lower than that of female life expectancy.

It is clear that various other factors beyond the level of development affect the magnitude of female over male difference in life expectancy. For cross-section analysis at the country level we have used three variables as indications of the level of development around 2010: rank for GDP per capita (World Bank data from the Human Development Report), rank for the Human Development Index (UNDP, 2011), and rank for life expectancy for females. Over the whole range of 168–196 countries (depending on the available data) there was no significant correlation with the female-male difference in life expectancy with all three indicators.

The international ordering by life expectancy at birth might be rather different for females and males. These differences in Table 4 are rather striking for two groups of countries, one with high negative and one with high positive difference between ranks for females and ranks for males, and a number of countries where this difference in ranks against the international position is not so pronounced. This would be hidden if one would calculate ranks for total life expectancy only.

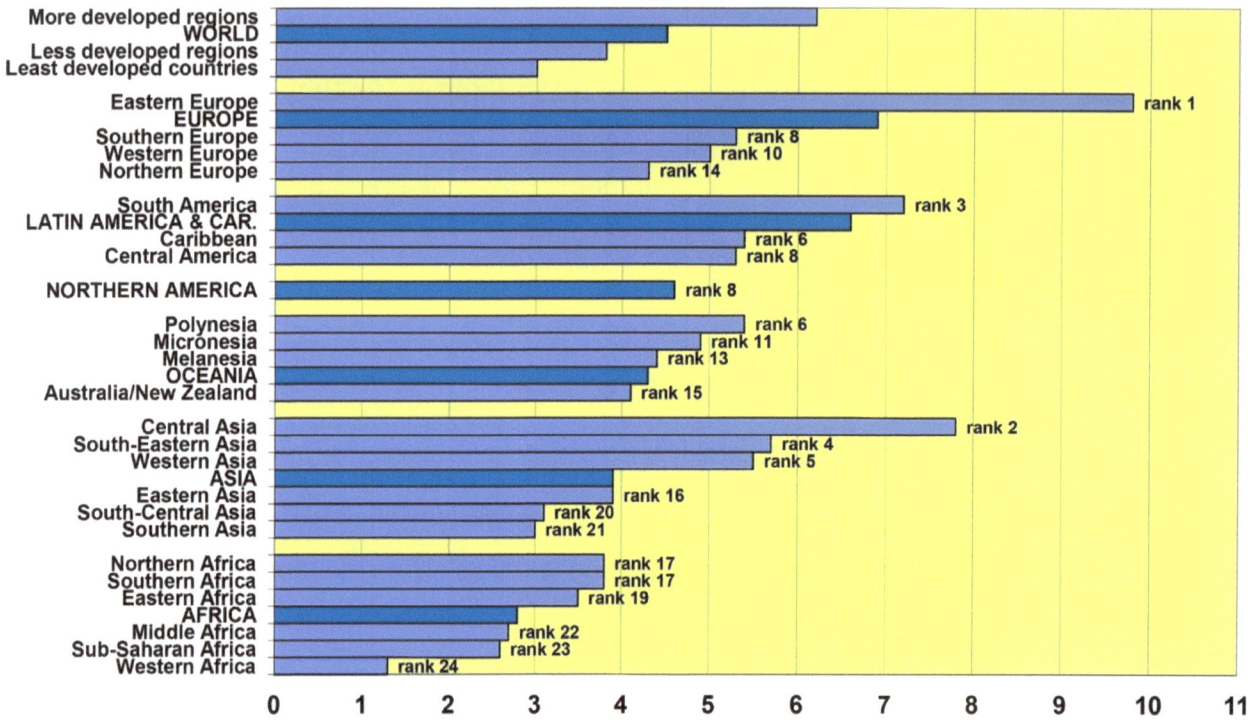

FIGURE 5 Gender disparities in life expectancy at birth for world regions in 2015
SOURCE: Calculation based on data from UN (2015).

Table 4 shows the results for the two groups of countries for which the difference of female and male rankings is 20 ranks or more, either negative or positive. The extreme negative differences of more than 50 ranks is shown for Lithuania, e.g. the rank of Lithuania against the international position for females was 62, while the corresponding rank for males was 120. On the other extreme of positive differences e.g. the rank for Iran was 101 for females and only 56 for males. A more complex analysis of various reasons for such extreme difference is needed; including general and specific country factors as these outcomes offer an interesting starting point. The unweighted average of the female-male life expectancy gap of the 20 countries in the first group was 9.1 years and that for the second group of 18 countries was 2.8 years.

In addition to the analysis of the ranks, in the last column in Table 4 the relative position of the countries in the two groups is evaluated by the S-time-distance for total life expectancy against the international frontier of the ten best countries in the world for the respective gender at a given point in time.

The average value of S-time-distance behind the international frontier is 43 years for the first group with negative values of difference in ranks (rank females minus rank males), i.e. for the countries where the life expectancy for females ranks much better than that of males. For the second group with positive values of difference in ranks (rank females minus rank males), i.e. for the countries where the life expectancy for males ranks much better than that of females; the total life expectancy for this group is on the average 41 years behind the international frontier. With the exception of one country time distances behind international frontier were more than 10 years, which points to the fact that these groups of countries do not belong to the top group of the most developed countries.

Country	FEMALES		MALES		Difference between female and male life expectancy (years)	Difference in ranks (rank females minus rank males)	S-time-distance from international frontier for both genders (in years)
	Life expectancy at birth (years)	Rank Females	Life expectancy at birth (years)	Rank Males			
Lithuania	79.1	62	67.9	120	11.2	-58	43.5
Syrian Arab	76.6	102	63.9	153	12.7	-51	(66)
Latvia	79	64	69.3	111	9.7	-47	40
Belarus	77.3	97	65.7	138	11.6	-41	59
Russian Federation	75.9	106	64.6	146	11.3	-40	63.7
Viet Nam	80.6	53	71.2	93	9.4	-40	33.5
Venezuela	78.6	70	70.4	107	8.2	-37	39.5
Estonia	81.4	47	72.2	83	9.2	-36	27.5
Seychelles	78.2	78	69.1	113	9.1	-35	44.5
Ukraine	76	103	66.2	137	9.8	-34	61
Armenia	78.7	67	71.1	94	7.6	-27	37.5
Puerto Rico	83.5	24	75.8	50	7.7	-26	15
Brazil	78.5	73	71	98	7.5	-25	38.3
Kazakhstan	74.3	121	64.8	145	9.5	-24	(66)
El Salvador	77.7	92	68.6	115	9.1	-23	44.5
Guadeloupe	84.5	12	77.7	35	6.8	-23	9
Argentina	80.2	55	72.6	77	7.6	-22	30
Hungary	78.8	66	71.6	88	7.2	-22	36
Turkmenistan	70	143	61.6	165	8.4	-22	(80)
Poland	81.5	45	73.6	65	7.9	-20	24.5
Malaysia	77.3	97	72.6	77	4.7	20	37.5
Malta	82.4	38	79	18	3.4	20	11
Nepal	71.5	135	68.6	115	2.9	20	65
Tunisia	77.4	96	72.7	74	4.7	22	37
U. A. Emirates	78.7	67	76.5	45	2.2	22	27
Micronesia	70.3	141	68.2	118	2.1	23	(68)
State of Palestine	75.1	117	71.1	94	4	23	45.5
Cabo Verde	75.2	114	71.6	88	3.6	26	43.5
Bangladesh	73.3	130	70.7	103	2.6	27	55
Jordan	75.9	106	72.6	77	3.3	29	40.3
Bhutan	70.1	142	69.6	110	0.5	32	(65)
Saudi Arabia	75.9	106	73.2	71	2.7	35	39.5
China	77.5	93	74.5	56	3	37	33
Maldives	78	84	76	47	2	37	27.5
Bahrain	77.8	89	75.9	48	1.9	41	29
Kuwait	75.9	106	73.6	65	2.3	41	39
Morocco	75.3	113	73.3	69	2	44	40
Iran	76.7	101	74.5	56	2.2	45	34.7

TABLE 4 Countries where the differences between female ranks and male ranks were more than 20 ranks in 2015 and time distances from international frontier for both genders
NOTES: The values of S-time-distance in the brackets are estimated by extrapolation of international frontier.
SOURCE: Data from UN (2015) and own calculations based on this data.

This brief analysis of disparities in the world for female and male life expectancy against the respective benchmarks opens an important background for the discussion of world disparities in life expectancy and female-male disparities.

Comparing five levels of analysis of gender disparities

Table 5 from Sicherl (2014b) compares five levels of analysis of gender disparities: female-male differences in life expectancy at birth for world average, for the average of EU27, for averages of two regional disaggregation in the EU, and for the average of more than 3000 USA counties. It has been shown that that the values of absolute differences between female and male life expectancy are for quartiles similar for the EU and USA cases. However, the S-time-distances between the trends of levels of female and male life expectancy in 2008 were 28 years for the EU27 and 35 years for the USA; in both cases showing very substantial and persuading differences in favour of women in these two developed regions.

It is also of interest to note that in the EU and in the USA the upper value of absolute difference is very similar, at about 11 years. The lower limit is below 4 years for EU countries and larger regions; for finer disaggregation to NUTS2 regions in the EU and even finer to USA counties the lowest female-male differences for life expectancy start at 2.3 years and 2.7 years, respectively. The range of values for world countries -2.0 to 12.5 is wider, but the world average is smaller than for the two compared countries.

	World countries	EU27 countries	NUTS1	NUTS2	USA counties
	2005–2010	around 2010	around 2010	around 2010	2007
Number of units	196	27	97	269	3118
Range of absolute differences (years)	-2.0–12.5	3.9–10.9	3.8–10.9	2.3–10.9	2.7–11.1
Average females-males (years)	4.6 (4.4)	6.3 (5.9)	5.9	5.8	5.6
Q1	2.8	4.8	4.5	4.5	4.9
Q2	4.6	6.1	5.9	5.5	5.5
Q3	6.4	7.4	7	6.9	6.2

TABLE 5 Gender disparities in life expectancy at the world, EU27, and regional levels
NOTES: Values in brackets refer to the weighted values for the aggregate.
SOURCE: From Sicherl (2014b), calculation based on data from UN (2011); Eurostat (2012a, 2012b); Kulkarni et al. (2011).

Chapter 3

GENDER DISPARITIES IN EU28 COUNTRIES

Female-male disparity in life expectancy at birth for EU28 countries

In this chapter we show the degree of inequality in female life expectancy between EU28 countries by showing tables of S-time-matrix, S-time-distance, and S-time-step as indicated in the methodology in Chapter 2. It is done first for demonstrating how differences between countries would look like for females before undertaking female-male differences in life expectancy at birth.

LEVEL	61	62	63	64	65	66	67	68	69	70	71	72	73	74	75	76	77	78	79	80	81	82	83	84	85
INT FRONT												1950	1953	1957	1963	1969	1974	1977	1981	1987	1992	1998	2002	2007	2012
EU28								1952	1954	1956	1958	1961	1964	1970	1974	1979	1983	1988	1994	1999	2003	2007	2013		
Italy							1951	1952	1954	1956	1959	1962	1965	1969	1972	1975	1979	1982	1986	1990	1994	1999	2003	2007	2012
Spain					1950	1952	1953	1955	1956	1958	1960	1962	1965	1968	1971	1975	1977	1980	1983	1987	1992	1997	2002	2006	2012
France									1951	1953	1954	1957	1959	1962	1967	1972	1975	1979	1983	1987	1991	1996	2002	2007	2013
Luxembourg										1952	1955	1958	1961	1966	1973	1977	1981	1984	1987	1992	1997	2001	2007	2010	2015
Austria									1951	1953	1955	1958	1961	1965	1972	1976	1980	1984	1988	1992	1996	2000	2004	2009	2015
Greece									1954	1956	1959	1961	1965	1968	1971	1975	1978	1981	1983	1988	1993	1998	2004	2010	2015
Portugal			1952	1954	1956	1959	1961	1963	1965	1967	1969	1972	1974	1976	1978	1981	1983	1986	1991	1996	2000	2004	2008	2011	2015
Sweden														1952	1955	1960	1966	1970	1975	1981	1987	1994	2000	2007	2015
Finland										1952	1954	1957	1960	1966	1970	1973	1975	1978	1981	1990	1995	2000	2004	2009	
Netherlands														1952	1955	1959	1964	1972	1976	1980	1989	1994	2003	2007	2012
Slovenia							1950	1952	1954	1956	1959	1963	1970	1974	1980	1986	1990	1994	1997	2001	2004	2008	2012		
Belgium												1952	1955	1957	1961	1969	1974	1978	1982	1986	1990	1995	2001	2007	2013
Germany											1951	1954	1956	1960	1965	1972	1976	1980	1984	1988	1993	1997	2001	2006	2012
Ireland							1951	1952	1954	1956	1958	1962	1967	1974	1979	1983	1987	1992	1999	2002	2005	2008	2014		
United Kingdom												1950	1953	1956	1963	1970	1978	1983	1988	1994	2000	2004	2010		
Cyprus								1951	1953	1956	1958	1961	1964	1968	1972	1976	1981	1987	1993	1999	2007	2012			
Malta							1951	1953	1955	1958	1962	1966	1970	1974	1978	1982	1987	1992	1997	2002	2007	2013			
Denmark												1952	1955	1959	1966	1971	1976	1993	2000	2004	2008	2013			
Czech Republic							1950	1952	1953	1954	1955	1957	1960	1977	1988	1992	1996	2000	2004	2008	2012				
Poland			1951	1952	1953	1954	1956	1957	1958	1960	1962	1964	1968	1973	1982	1994	1997	2000	2004	2008	2012				
Estonia			1950	1951	1952	1953	1954	1955	1956	1957	1958	1960	1962	1967	1997	2000	2002	2005	2007	2010	2013				
Croatia			1950	1952	1954	1956	1958	1960	1961	1963	1966	1968	1970	1973	1977	1985	1990	1994	1998	2005	2010				
Slovakia				1950	1951	1952	1953	1954	1955	1956	1958	1960	1963	1976	1986	1993	1998	2004	2009	2015					
Lithuania	1950	1951	1952	1952	1953	1954	1955	1955	1956	1958	1959	1960	1962	1965	1969	1997	2001	2009	2015						
Latvia				1951	1952	1953	1953	1954	1955	1958	1959	1961	1996	1999	2002	2007	2010	2015							
Hungary				1951	1952	1954	1955	1957	1960	1962	1967	1982	1992	1996	2000	2003	2008								
Romania			1954	1956	1957	1958	1959	1961	1962	1968	1972	1977	1991	1999	2002	2005	2008	2013							
Bulgaria		1950	1952	1953	1954	1955	1956	1957	1959	1960	1961	1963	1967	1981	2000	2005	2009								

FIGURE 6 Time matrix for female life expectancy for EU28 countries
SOURCE: Own calculation based on data from UN (2015).

There is a wealth of information in these tables; very many possible comparisons are not discussed here in detail. While in France, Spain, and Italy the female life expectancy already reached 85 years, in Romania and Bulgaria was around 77-78 years, a difference of 8-7 years. At a glance one can see that even in the EU28 there are substantial differences in female life expectancy between the member countries.

Comparing the rows for EU28 average and for the international frontier in Figures 7 and 9 one can immediately see that international frontier has passed through less levels than EU28 average and that given levels of female life expectancy were attained earlier by the average of the 10 best countries forming international frontier than for EU28 average, which is lagging for about 11 years.

At the level of female life expectancy of 84 years only Spain was ahead of the international frontier average, being 0.5 years ahead. Twelve EU countries lagged the international frontier from 7 to 12 years, another 13 countries lagged from 14.5 years in Cyprus to 35.5 years in Bulgaria.

LEVEL	72	73	74	75	76	77	78	79	80	81	82	83	84	85
INT FRONT	0	0	0	0	0	0	0	0	0	0	0	0	0	0
EU28	11	11	13	11	10	10	11	13	12	11	10	11		
Italy	12	12	12	9	6	5	5	5	3	2	1	1	1	0
Spain	12	11	11	8	6	4	3	2	1	0	-1	0	-1	1
France	7	6	5	4	3	2	2	2	1	-1	-2	0	0	2
Luxembourg	11	12	16	14	12	11	10	11	10	9	9	8	8	
Austria	11	12	15	13	11	11	11	11	9	8	7	7	9	
Greece	15	15	14	12	9	7	6	7	6	6	7	8	9	
Portugal	24	23	21	18	14	13	14	15	14	12	10	9	9	
Sweden		-1	-2	-3	-4	-4	-2	-1	1	2	3	5	9	
Finland	10	12	13	10	6	4	4	9	9	8	7	7		
Netherlands		-2	-2	-4	-5	-2	-1	-1	3	11	10	10		
Slovenia	13	17	17	17	17	16	17	16	15	12	10	10		
Belgium	7	8	12	11	9	9	9	9	8	9	9	11		
Germany	10	12	15	13	11	10	11	12	10	9	8	10		
Ireland	12	14	17	16	14	14	15	18	16	13	11	12		
United Kingdom	3	3	6	7	9	9	11	13	14	12	12			
Cyprus	11	11	11	9	7	8	10	12	13	15	15			
Malta	16	16	17	15	13	14	15	16	15	15	15			
Denmark	2	1	2	3	2	2	16	19	18	16	16			
Czech Republic	7	7	20	25	23	23	23	23	21	20				
Poland	14	14	16	19	25	24	23	23	22	20				
Estonia	10	9	10	34	31	29	28	26	23	21				
Croatia	20	20	20	22	21	21	21	24	24					
Slovakia	10	9	19	23	24	25	27	28	29					
Lithuania	10	9	8	6	28	27	32	34						
Latvia	9	8	39	36	33	34	33	34						
Hungary	17	29	35	33	31	30	31							
Romania	27	38	42	39	36	35	36							
Bulgaria	13	14	24	37	36	36								

FIGURE 7 S-time-distance lag in years behind international frontier for females
SOURCE: Own calculation based on Figure 6.

The earlier discussion of the female-male differences in life expectancy can be analysed also separately for women and men in terms of time distance lagging behind the international frontier of the average of 10 world best countries (see Sicherl, 2014b for earlier results).

The more detailed estimates of the dynamics used by the S-time-step measure are presented in Figure 8. The values of S-time-step show the number of years needed in the past to reach the next consecutive level of female life expectancy. The average value of S-time-step in the row for EU28 is 4.1 years, i.e. in the past about 4 years were needed for increase in 1 year of life expectancy over the analysed period. Portugal shows the highest dynamics.

What is clear is that there are astonishing differences in gender life expectancy between EU countries. To examine this we calculated ranks separately for females and males against the world list of 200 countries from data in UN (2015) and the respective differences between the two ranks. There are only 10 countries for which the absolute difference in the ranking is lower than 10. In the world context Italy stands out from the EU countries as it is ranked 4 for both genders. Spain is placed at 5 for females, but at 12 for males, France showed a similar difference 6 for females and 16 for males; for Sweden this is reversed, at 17 for females and 6 for males.

LEVEL	61	62	63	64	65	66	67	68	69	70	71	72	73	74	75	76	77	78	79	80	81	82	83	84	85
INT FRONT													3.3	3.7	6.0	6.0	4.5	3.5	4.0	5.5	5.5	5.5	4.5	4.5	5.0
EU28									1.9	2.0	2.4	2.7	3.3	5.5	4.5	4.5	4.5	5.0	5.5	5.0	4.2	4.3	5.5		
Italy								1.8	1.7	2.0	2.5	3.2	3.3	3.7	3.3	3.3	3.3	3.7	3.3	4.0	4.3	4.5	4.0	4.5	4.5
Spain						1.6	1.3	1.4	1.6	1.7	1.8	2.2	2.7	3.2	3.7	3.2	2.8	2.5	2.9	4.3	5.0	5.0	5.0	4.0	6.0
France									1.9	1.8	2.1	2.5	3.0	5.0	4.7	3.7	3.7	4.3	3.7	4.0	5.0	5.7	4.8	6.5	
Luxembourg									2.9	2.8	3.0	4.5	7.5	4.0	4.0	3.0	3.0	4.5	5.0	4.5	5.5	3.8	4.2		
Austria								2.5	2.3	2.5	2.8	4.5	7.0	4.3	4.0	3.7	3.5	4.0	4.2	4.3	4.0	5.0	6.0		
Greece								2.6	2.5	2.5	3.3	3.8	2.9	3.3	3.5	2.5	2.8	4.2	5.0	5.5	6.0	6.3	4.7		
Portugal			2.5	2.2	2.2	2.0	2.2	2.0	2.2	2.3	2.5	2.3	2.2	2.0	2.3	2.5	3.0	5.0	4.5	4.5	4.0	3.7	3.3	4.0	
Sweden													3.3	4.7	5.5	4.5	5.0	5.5	6.5	6.5	6.5	7.0	8.0		
Finland											2.2	2.7	3.3	5.5	4.2	2.8	2.5	2.8	3.3	9.0	5.0	4.5	4.5	5.0	
Netherlands													3.3	3.7	5.3	8.0	4.0	4.0	9.0	13.5	4.5	4.5			
Slovenia								2.0	1.9	2.0	2.5	3.8	7.5	4.3	5.7	5.5	4.0	4.5	3.3	3.7	3.3	3.2	4.0		
Belgium											2.3	2.5	4.0	7.5	5.5	4.0	4.0	3.7	4.0	4.8	6.5	5.5	6.0		
Germany										2.5	2.8	3.7	5.0	7.0	4.3	3.7	3.7	3.8	5.0	4.0	4.2	4.8	6.5		
Ireland								1.5	1.5	2.0	2.5	3.4	5.3	7.0	4.5	4.0	4.5	5.0	6.5	3.5	2.8	3.3	6.0		
United Kingdom													3.0	3.3	6.2	7.5	7.5	5.0	5.5	6.0	6.0	4.3	5.2		
Cyprus										2.5	2.3	2.8	2.8	3.3	3.3	3.8	4.5	5.0	5.5	6.0	6.5	7.5	5.5		
Malta									2.3	2.5	3.1	3.3	4.0	3.8	4.0	4.5	4.3	4.7	4.5	5.0	5.0	5.5	5.5		
Denmark													2.9	4.3	7.0	4.7	4.8	17.5	7.0	4.3	4.0	4.7			
Czech Republic								1.5	1.1	1.3	1.4	1.9	2.8	16.5	11.0	4.5	4.0	3.7	4.0	3.8	4.0				
Poland			0.9	1.0	1.1	1.2	1.3	1.4	1.7	2.0	2.3	3.3	4.8	9.5	12.0	3.3	2.8	3.7	4.3	4.0					
Estonia		1.1	0.7	0.8	0.9	0.9	1.0	1.2	1.3	1.8	2.3	4.2	30.2	3.0	2.6	2.8	2.3	2.5	2.9						
Croatia		2.0	1.7	1.8	1.8	1.9	1.8	2.0	2.2	2.2	2.5	2.8	4.0	8.0	5.0	4.0	3.5	7.8	4.7						
Slovakia				1.3	0.9	0.9	1.0	1.0	1.3	1.3	1.9	2.9	13.5	10.0	7.0	5.0	6.0	5.0	6.0						
Lithuania	1.0	0.6	0.6	0.7	0.8	0.8	0.8	1.0	1.1	1.3	1.6	1.9	2.5	4.3	28.0	3.5	8.5	5.5							
Latvia				0.7	0.8	0.8	0.9	1.0	1.1	1.2	1.6	1.8	34.5	3.5	3.3	4.7	3.3	4.7							
Hungary						1.5	1.5	1.6	1.8	2.3	2.8	4.7	15.0	9.5	4.5	3.7	3.7	4.7							
Romania				1.8	1.4	1.1	1.1	1.2	1.4	6.0	4.0	5.0	14.0	3.0	3.0	3.3	4.2								
Bulgaria		1.5	1.1	1.1	1.1	1.1	1.1	1.2	1.3	1.4	1.8	4.0	14.0	19.0	4.5	4.5									

FIGURE 8 S-time-step (years): time needed to achieve the next level of the life expectancy for the females

SOURCE: Own calculation based on Figure 6.

Surprisingly high differences in ranking in Table 6 are found in five countries in the table, indicating that the world ranks for male life expectancy are much worse than that for females. For Estonia, Latvia and Lithuania the difference between the two rankings favour females by more than 35 ranks; e.g. Estonia occupies rank 47 for female and 83 for male life expectancy. The position of women in society over a long period, history and also the lifestyle of men might be influencing these differences in the rankings. Contrasting cases in the other direction are Malta, Ireland, and the United Kingdom.

The method of calculating S-time-distances in Table 6 is slightly different from that earlier using the time matrix in Figure 2. The level of male life expectancy for 2015 is the starting point, and it is calculated at what time in the time series for females for the corresponding unit this value has been reached. The differences between the two procedures are small and do not affect the general conclusions. The third column in Table 6 shows the time lag for males behind females for life expectancy at birth. S-time-distance shows a much higher degree of gender disparity than the static measures; the time delay ranges from 17 years for Ireland to 60 years for Lithuania.

Level	60	61	62	63	64	65	66	67	68	69	70	71	72	73	74	75	76	77	78	79	80	81	82	83	84	85
INT FRONT F													1950	1953	1957	1963	1969	1974	1977	1981	1987	1992	1998	2002	2007	2012
INT FRONT M										1954	1964	1972	1977	1982	1987	1992	1997	2000	2004	2008	2012					
EU28 F									1952	1954	1956	1958	1961	1964	1970	1974	1979	1983	1988	1994	1999	2003	2007	2013		
EU28 M				1950	1953	1955	1958	1962	1970	1977	1983	1988	1994	1997	2001	2004	2007	2011	2015							
Italy F								1951	1952	1954	1956	1959	1962	1965	1969	1972	1975	1979	1982	1986	1990	1994	1999	2003	2007	2012
Spain F				1950	1952	1953	1955	1956	1958	1960	1962	1965	1968	1971	1975	1977	1980	1983	1987	1992	1997	2002	2006	2012		
France F									1951	1953	1954	1957	1959	1962	1967	1972	1975	1979	1983	1987	1991	1996	2002	2007	2013	
Luxembourg F										1952	1955	1958	1961	1966	1973	1977	1981	1984	1987	1992	1997	2001	2007	2010	2015	
Austria F								1951	1953	1955	1958	1961	1965	1972	1976	1980	1984	1988	1992	1996	2000	2004	2009	2015		
Greece F								1954	1956	1959	1961	1965	1968	1971	1975	1978	1981	1983	1988	1993	1998	2004	2010	2015		
Portugal F			1952	1954	1956	1959	1961	1963	1965	1967	1969	1972	1974	1976	1978	1981	1983	1986	1991	1996	2000	2004	2008	2011	2015	
Sweden F														1952	1955	1960	1966	1970	1975	1981	1987	1994	2000	2007	2015	
Finland F										1952	1954	1957	1960	1966	1970	1973	1975	1978	1981	1990	1995	2000	2004	2009		
Netherlands F														1952	1955	1959	1964	1972	1976	1980	1989	2003	2007	2012		
Slovenia F							1950	1952	1954	1956	1959	1963	1970	1974	1980	1986	1990	1994	1997	2001	2004	2008	2012			
Germany F									1951	1954	1956	1960	1965	1972	1976	1980	1984	1988	1993	1997	2001	2006	2012			
Belgium F										1952	1955	1957	1961	1969	1974	1978	1982	1986	1990	1995	2001	2007	2013			
Ireland F								1951	1952	1954	1956	1958	1962	1967	1974	1979	1983	1987	1992	1999	2002	2005	2008	2014		
United Kingdom F													1950	1953	1956	1963	1970	1978	1983	1988	1994	2000	2004	2010		
Cyprus F								1951	1953	1956	1958	1961	1964	1968	1972	1976	1981	1987	1993	1999	2007	2012				
Malta F								1951	1953	1955	1958	1962	1966	1970	1974	1978	1982	1987	1992	1997	2002	2007	2013			
Denmark F														1952	1955	1959	1966	1971	1976	1993	2000	2004	2008	2013		
Czech Republic F							1950	1952	1953	1954	1955	1957	1960	1977	1988	1992	1996	2000	2004	2008	2012					
Poland F				1951	1952	1953	1954	1956	1957	1958	1960	1962	1964	1968	1973	1982	1994	1997	2000	2004	2008	2012				
Estonia F				1950	1951	1952	1953	1954	1955	1956	1957	1958	1960	1962	1967	1997	2000	2002	2005	2007	2010	2013				
Croatia F			1950	1952	1954	1956	1958	1960	1961	1963	1966	1968	1970	1973	1977	1985	1990	1994	1998	2005	2010					
Italy M				1952	1954	1958	1963	1968	1972	1977	1981	1984	1988	1993	1996	1999	2002	2005	2008	2012						
Sweden M												1951	1956	1971	1981	1987	1991	1995	1999	2003	2008	2012				
Slovakia F				1950	1951	1952	1953	1954	1955	1956	1958	1960	1963	1976	1986	1993	1998	2004	2009	2015						
Spain M		1951	1953	1954	1956	1957	1959	1962	1966	1970	1974	1977	1980	1984	1994	1998	2002	2005	2008	2011	2015					
Netherlands M											1970	1978	1984	1991	1997	2002	2005	2008	2011							
Luxembourg M				1952	1955	1959	1963	1974	1978	1982	1985	1988	1992	1995	1999	2002	2005	2008	2010	2013						
France M				1952	1955	1958	1962	1970	1975	1980	1984	1988	1992	1996	2000	2003	2006	2010	2013							
Lithuania F		1950	1951	1952	1952	1953	1954	1955	1955	1956	1958	1959	1960	1962	1965	1969	1997	2001	2009	2015						
Austria M					1955	1958	1962	1972	1977	1981	1984	1987	1990	1994	1997	2000	2003	2007	2011	2015						
Ireland M				1952	1954	1956	1961	1975	1981	1986	1990	1996	2000	2002	2005	2007	2011	2015								
Latvia F				1951	1952	1953	1953	1954	1955	1956	1958	1959	1961	1996	1999	2002	2007	2010	2015							
Malta M				1951	1954	1958	1961	1964	1968	1972	1976	1980	1984	1989	1994	1999	2004	2010	2015							
Hungary F				1951	1952	1955	1957	1960	1962	1967	1982	1992	1996	2000	2003	2008										
United Kingdom M								1954	1962	1973	1978	1983	1987	1991	1995	1999	2002	2006	2010							
Germany M					1951	1956	1962	1973	1978	1982	1985	1990	1995	1998	2001	2004	2007	2012								
Romania F				1954	1956	1957	1958	1959	1961	1962	1968	1972	1977	1991	1999	2002	2005	2008	2013							
Belgium M					1952	1955	1959	1971	1976	1981	1985	1989	1993	1998	2002	2005	2009	2013								
Denmark M								1954	1974	1989	1995	1999	2003	2006	2009	2013										
Cyprus M					1950	1953	1956	1958	1961	1964	1968	1972	1976	1981	1987	1993	2001	2009	2014							
Finland M			1951	1953	1956	1959	1970	1974	1977	1980	1983	1990	1993	1997	2000	2003	2007	2011	2014							
Greece M					1955	1958	1960	1964	1969	1972	1977	1981	1985	1988	1991	1994	2001	2006	2014							
Portugal M	1960	1962	1965	1968	1970	1973	1976	1979	1981	1983	1986	1992	1997	2000	2003	2006	2009	2012	2014							
Bulgaria F			1950	1952	1953	1954	1955	1956	1957	1959	1960	1961	1963	1967	1981	2000	2005	2009								
Slovenia M			1950	1952	1955	1957	1973	1980	1986	1990	1993	1997	2000	2003	2005	2007	2010	2013								
Czech Republic M				1951	1953	1954	1956	1978	1990	1994	1996	1999	2002	2006	2008	2011										
Croatia M	1954	1957	1960	1963	1967	1972	1980	1984	1987	1992	1995	1999	2005	2010	2014											
Poland M	1954	1955	1956	1957	1959	1962	1965	1993	1997	1999	2002	2006	2010	2013												
Slovakia M		1951	1952	1953	1954	1955	1956	1989	1995	1999	2004	2008	2012													
Estonia M	1955	1956	1957	1996	1999	2001	2003	2005	2007	2008	2010	2012	2014													
Hungary M		1951	1953	1954	1956	1992	1996	1999	2002	2005	2008	2012														
Romania M	1955	1957	1958	1959	1960	1962	1997	2001	2003	2006	2009	2013														
Bulgaria M	1952	1953	1954	1955	1957	1958	1959	1960	2000	2005	2010															
Latvia M	1954	1955	1996	1998	2000	2003	2007	2009	2011	2014																
Lithuania M	1954	1955	1956	1957	1995	1999	2010	2012																		

Females		Males

FIGURE 9 Time matrix containing both female (F) and male (M) life expectances for EU countries

NOTE: International frontier F (females) and international frontier M (males) represent the unweighted average of the best 10 countries in the world for life expectancy for each year in UN (2015) for the respective gender.

SOURCE: Own calculation based on data from UN (2015).

Figure 9 presents a large time matrix combining female and male life expectancy for all EU28 countries over the analysed period. It is a clear visualisation over many units and over time that offers a condensed summary at a glance. This time matrix condenses information of combined tables of time series of female and male life expectancy for the period of more than 65 years (1950-2015), which in UN (2015) data amounts to about 3700 entries; in this time matrix it is condensed to much smaller number of entries (about 850). This presents a first level visualisation that usefully complements the details in the original database by showing the easily understandable summary overview.

Country	Difference between female and male life expectancy (years) in 2015	Gender difference as a percentage of male life expectancy	S-time-distance: Time lag for males behind females in life expectancy	World rank for females 2015	World rank for males 2015	Difference in ranks (females minus males)
Sweden	3.4	4.2%	24	17	6	11
Malta	3.4	4.3%	19	38	18	20
Netherlands	3.6	4.5%	28	24	13	11
Denmark	3.8	4.8%	18	39	27	12
United Kingdom	3.8	4.8%	22	35	21	14
Ireland	4.1	5.2%	17	32	18	14
Cyprus	4.4	5.6%	28	37	29	8
Luxembourg	4.5	5.7%	21	15	15	0
Germany	4.7	6.0%	24	27	24	3
Italy	4.8	5.9%	21	4	4	0
Austria	4.9	6.2%	23	17	17	0
Belgium	4.9	6.2%	27	27	27	0
Spain	5.4	6.8%	28	5	12	-7
Finland	5.6	7.2%	33	21	29	-8
Czech Republic	5.7	7.5%	23	42	48	-6
France	5.8	7.3%	30	6	16	-10
Greece	5.8	7.4%	31	17	29	-12
Portugal	5.8	7.4%	23	17	29	-12
Slovenia	5.9	7.6%	23	24	36	-12
Croatia	6.6	8.9%	37	51	59	-8
Bulgaria	6.9	9.7%	54	89	100	-11
Romania	7.1	10.0%	42	76	90	-14
Hungary	7.2	10.1%	50	66	88	-22
Slovakia	7.3	10.0%	54	57	74	-17
Poland	7.9	10.7%	45	45	65	-20
Estonia	9.2	12.7%	55	47	83	-36
Latvia	9.7	14.0%	59	64	111	-47
Lithuania	11.2	16.5%	60	62	120	-58
EU28	5.3	6.8%	26			

TABLE 6 Female-male disparity in life expectancy at birth for EU28 countries
SOURCE: Own calculation based on data from UN (2015).

Overall it is easy to observe that the female time series have reached much higher values than that for males. Women life expectancy is higher than that of males in all EU countries (easily observed if we would arrange the rows as for EU28 F and EU28 M). This tendency is so strong that the first 22 positions in Figure 9 ordered by the value of life expectancy are that of female life expectancy. Only in six countries (Slovakia, Lithuania, Hungary, Latvia, Romania, and Bulgaria) the female life expectancy was mixed with the male life expectancy among some above average EU countries.

This large combined time matrix enables comparisons across gender within a group as well as comparisons of levels of either female or male life expectancy between different units used in the figure. The choice between these possibilities depends on the analytical priority of the user.

If one would be concerned predominantly with gender differences within countries the arrangement in the upper part for EU28 averages for female and male values (or between the values for the international frontier) would be easier to observe gender disparities directly. Only for the span of life expectancy between 68 and 78 years values for both genders are available, and for these values the rounded S-time-distances amount from 18 to 33 years of lag of male life expectancy behind female life expectancy (i.e. so many years earlier have these levels for males been achieved by females).

The time matrix format with the table-graph characteristics allows at the same time two types of comparisons between countries and genders and calculation of corresponding differences between countries and genders. First, visually one can observe which approximate levels were achieved over the period as well as the dynamics in terms of the number of steps in life expectancy achieved (depending on the data available). Second, from the values of times in the time matrix further measures can be calculated, i.e. S-time-distances between genders and countries, on the one hand, and S-time-steps as additional measure of dynamics, on the other. Out of a very large number of possible comparisons in Figure 9 only a small number of available comparisons can be commented here.

Figure 10 shows the results of S-time-distance delays of male life expectancy behind female life expectancy over the analysed period. The general conclusion is that the time distance perspective indicates that in the past the gender difference in life expectancy in the EU has been very large and rather stable.

Both for the averages for the international frontier and for the EU28 average it is shown that the average time delay was at about 27-28 years; the relationship is very persistent and it changes very slowly. Broadly speaking, at the lower end of the table there are 10 countries with S-time-distance delay of more than 30 years, for five of them (Estonia, Slovakia, Lithuania, Latvia, and Bulgaria) the time delay of male behind the female life expectancy is more than 50 years, i.e. more than half a century.

Overall conclusion is that the time distance method significantly showed the large time distance perspective of the degree of disparity between female and male life expectancy that is not taken into account in the standard static analysis of disparities.

Level	66	67	68	69	70	71	72	73	74	75	76	77	78	79	80
Inter. frontier M							27	29	30	29	28	27	27	27	25
EU28 M			18	23	27	30	33	33	31	30	29	28	27		
Italy M		13	16	18	21	23	23	23	24	24	24	23	23	23	22
Spain M	8	9	11	14	16	17	18	20	26	27	27	28	28	28	28
France M				24	27	30	32	33	34	33	32	31	31	30	
Luxembourg M				29	30	30	31	30	26	25	24	24	23	22	
Austria M			26	28	29	29	30	29	25	24	23	23	23	23	
Greece M			15	16	18	20	21	20	20	20	23	26	31		
Portugal M	15	16	16	16	17	20	23	24	25	26	26	26	23		
Sweden M								29	31	31	30	29	28	27	25
Finland M			28	29	33	33	31	30	31	32	33	33			
Netherlands M								32	36	38	38	33	32	31	
Slovenia M		30	33	35	37	38	38	33	31	27	24	24			
Belgium M				28	30	32	32	29	28	27	27	27			
Germany M			27	28	29	30	30	26	24	24	24				
Ireland M				21	25	27	28	29	26	24	22	20	19	17	
United Kingdom M						33	34	35	33	29	25	23	22		
Cyprus M			10	11	13	14	15	17	19	22	25	28	28		
Malta M		10	11	12	13	14	14	15	15	16	16	17	18	19	
Denmark M								37	40	40	37	36	34	20	
Czech Republic M		28	38	41	42	44	45	46	32	24					
Poland M		38	40	40	42	44	45	45							
Estonia M	50	51	52	53	53	54	54								
Croatia M	22	24	26	29	29	31	35	37	37						
Slovakia M		36	41	44	47	51	52								
Lithuania M	56	57													
Latvia M	54	56	57	58											
Hungary M	44	45	46	48	49	49									
Romania M	38	41	42	44	41	41									
Bulgaria M			43	47	50										

FIGURE 10 S-time-distance (years): time lag for males (M) behind females in life expectancy
SOURCE: Own calculation based on data from Figure 9.

A more detailed analysis for reasons is very complex and requires a large systematic research project dealing with both medical and social factors. One line of factors contributing to such dominant statistical fact of higher female than male life expectancy is possible difference in our genes. An example of such studies is that looking at the tendency for females to outlive males in different species in the animal kingdom (Monash University, 2012). In addition to economic and social factors there are important differences in life style and time use.

In analysing the gender differences in life expectancy between the EU28 countries some obvious possible explanatory factors like Global Gender Gap index of World Economic Forum (Hausmann, Tyson, and Zahidi, 2011), women's voting rights (UNDP, 2007), or real adjusted gross disposable income of households per capita (Eurostat, 2012c) did not show high degree of association.

Chapter 4

MEAN BODY MASS INDEX, OBESITY, AND DIABETES

Gender differences in mean body mass index (BMI) in a broader perspective: static and time distance dimensions

The concept of time distance applies across variables, fields of concern, and units of comparison. Here we shall apply it to comparisons of differences between genders and show that the degree of disparities may be very different in static terms and in time.

For instance, for 2014 the mean BMI values for France were 26.1 for males and 24.4 for females. In this year the mean BMI for males was higher than for females for 1.7 in value in absolute terms and for about 7 in percentage terms. Comparing in time, for the female mean BMI of 24.4 in 2014 we look back at the trend for males, and that value was attained for males earlier (in 1977, mean BMI M 1977 = mean BMI F 2014). S-time-distance between female and male mean BMI is -37 years at the female mean BMI level for 2014 (1977-2014). For a proper perception of the gender disparities in mean BMI we need all three statistical measures.

Technically, calculating the time distance for cases when male values are ahead of female values we estimate the time when the female 2014 value for a given country or region is attained earlier in the time trend of male values. For the other case of female values being ahead, the male MBI values in 2014 is searched in the female time trend and subtract that time from 2014.

The availability of 200 country data over the four decades in the NCD Risk Factor Collaboration study makes it possible to describe the magnitude of gender disparities in the time dimension in addition of the usual static or percentage differences. For the female values of mean BMI in 2014 here the time when these values were attained on the trends of the male mean BMI is estimated. S-time-distance values range from more than 40 years of mean BMI values for males being ahead of mean BMI for females for Switzerland and Japan to more than 40 years of time lag in the opposite direction for 5 countries. This is a very different perception of the gender disparities in the countries as those of percentage differences at given point in time.

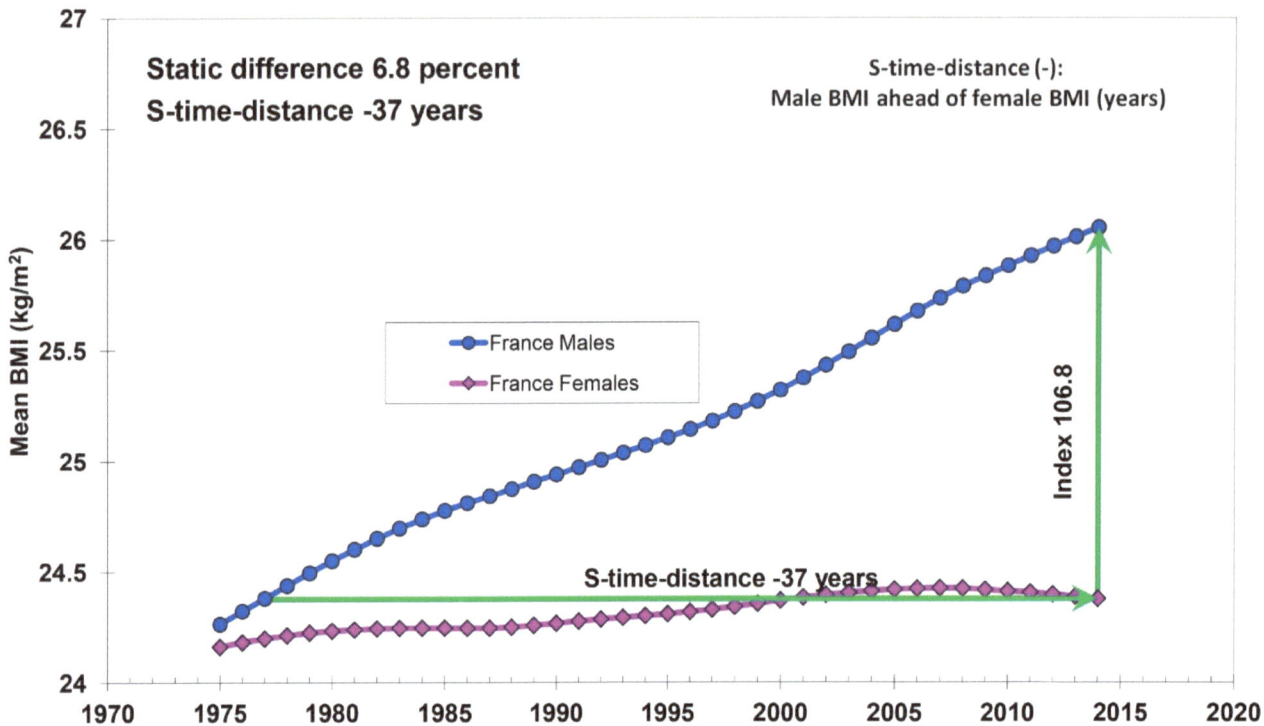

FIGURE 11 Gender disparities (male to female) in mean Body Mass Index (BMI): static index and time distance for 2014 in France

SOURCE: Own calculations based on data from NCD-RisC (2016c).

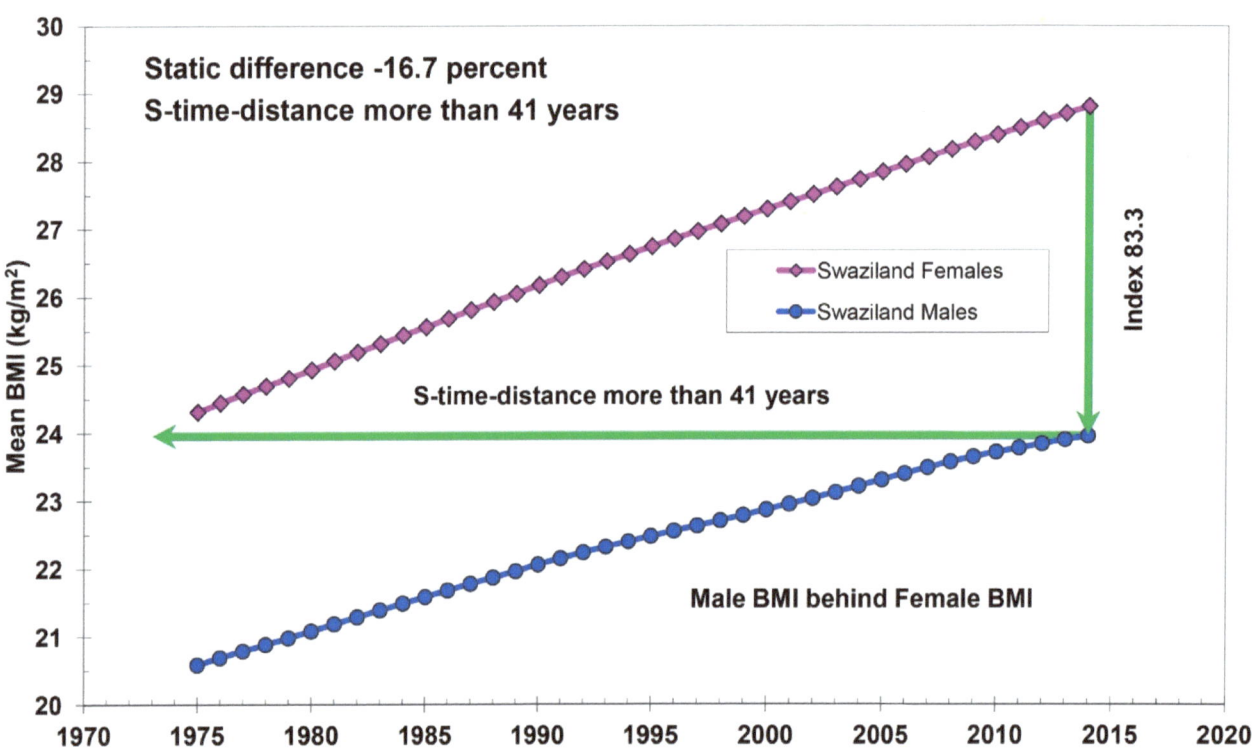

FIGURE 12 Gender disparities (male to female) in mean Body Mass Index (BMI): static index and time distance for 2014 in Swaziland

SOURCE: Own calculations based on data from NCD-RisC (2016c).

But the perception of the degree of differences may be very different. The perception based on percentage differences in 2014 (M/F) is moderate, from 11.8% higher for males in Switzerland to -16.7% for Swaziland. This overall range of percentages does not give the impression that the gender difference would be very difficult to change over time; while the S-time-distance between the mean BMI values for males and female of more than 40 years for Switzerland and more than 40 years in the other direction for Swaziland tell a very different story. We need both static and dynamic measures.

Looking at the long-term view with S-time-distances, in nearly one third of countries mean BMI for males was ahead of that for females, in nearly of two-third of countries mean BMI for females were ahead of mean BMI for males. It is interesting to note that the unweighted average of life expectancy in 20 countries with more than 20 years of time lead of male mean BMI ahead of female mean BMI was about 80.6 years, while for 45 countries at the other end with more than 20 years of time lag for male mean BMI behind female mean BMI was about 68.8 years. In other words, the countries with distinctly leading male mean BMI values are from the group of more developed countries as approximated by life expectancy.

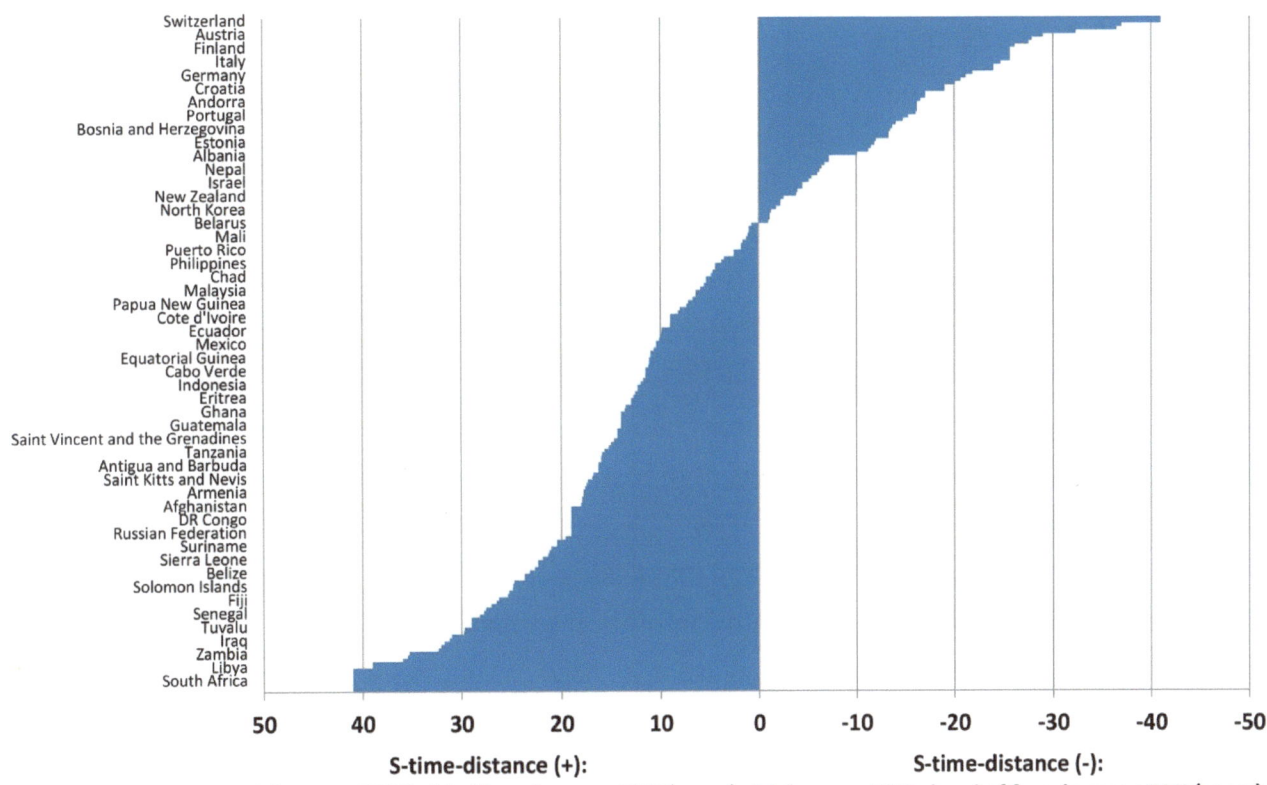

FIGURE 13 Comparing female and male levels of mean BMI in 2014
SOURCE: Own calculations based on data from NCD-RisC (2016c).

This is confirmed also by calculating S-time-distances for 9 mean BMI regional averages defined and available in the NCD Risk Collaboration database. For High-income Asia Pacific region the time lead for males was in 2014 about 30 years, for High-income Western countries about 11 years. Also for 24 EU countries the time lead was more than 10 years.

Mean BMI (kg/m2)	World			United States of America			United Kingdom			China			India			Egypt			Turkey			South Africa		
	Females	Males	S-time-distance	Females	Males	S-time-distance	Females	Males	S-time-distance	Females	Males	S-time-distance	Females	Males	S-time-distance	Females	Males	S-time-distance	Females	Males	S-time-distance	Females	Males	S-time-distance
30.5																2013								
30																2009								
29.5																2004								
29																2000								
28.5				2011	2008	-3										1995			2012			2011		
28				2006	2003	-2										1990			2005			2006		
27.5				2001	1999	-2										1986			1998			2001		
27				1997	1995	-2	2014	2007	-7							1982	2008	26	1992			1994		
26.5				1993	1991	-2	2005	2001	-4							1979	1997	19	1988	2007	19	1985		
26				1989	1986	-3	1999	1997	-3								1991		1984	2001	17	1977		
25.5				1985	1980	-5	1995	1992	-3								1986		1980	1997	17			
25				1980			1990	1987	-3								1982		1975	1993	17			
24.5							1986	1981	-5								1978		1989				2006	
24	2007	2011	4				1981				2012								1985				1999	
23.5	1999	2005	6				1976				2009								1981				1990	
23	1990	1997	7							2007	2005	-2							1977				1982	
22.5	1982	1988	6							2000	2000	0											1976	
22		1980								1989	1993	4												
21.5										1978	1985	7	2013											
21													2004	2007	2									
20.5													1997	1998	1									
20													1990	1989	0									
19.5													1984	1984	0									
19													1978	1979	1									

Legend: Females | Males | S-time-distance (-): Male mean BMI ahead of female mean BMI (years) | S-time-distance (+): Male mean BMI behind female mean BMI (years)

FIGURE 14 S-time-distance view of selected countries comparing female and male levels of mean BMI for the period 1975 - 2014

SOURCE: Own calculations based on data from NCD-RisC (2016c).

In five regions (South Asia, Latin America and Caribbean, Oceania, Sub-Saharan Africa, and Central Asia, Middle East and North Africa) female mean BMI values are ahead of male mean BMI, for the last two regions male values are lagging for about 20 years.

For gender differences between male and female mean BMI the range of percentage differences range from about 7% of higher male mean BMI for High-income Asia Pacific region and of about 7% lower male mean BMI in Sub-Saharan Africa, while the range of the time distance measure between the two regions shows the 30 years lead for males the former and about 20 years lag of males in the latter region. Again, both types of measures are needed to complement each other.

There is another way of presenting and visualising of the time series data. Time matrix is an original possibility of additional presentation of time series data. In the usual time series table data of the indicator (e.g. life expectancy) are organised in relation to the descriptors, like units (e.g. countries) and time (e.g. years). The time matrix presents the original data (or some approximations) in an alternative way: descriptors are units and levels of the indicator and the value in the field of the table are times when such levels were attained (see Sicherl 2015, Chapter 3).

Mean BMI (kg/m2)	Central and Eastern Europe			Central Asia, Middle East and North Africa			East and South East Asia			High-income Asia Pacific			High-income Western countries			Latin America and Caribbean			Oceania			South Asia			Sub-Saharan Africa		
	Females	Males	S-time-distance	Females	Males	S-time-distance	Females	Males	S-time-distance	Females	Males	S-time-distance	Females	Males	S-time-distance	Females	Males	S-time-distance	Females	Males	S-time-distance	Females	Males	S-time-distance	Females	Males	S-time-distance
27.5				2009										2010														
27				2004										2004		2014												
26.5				1997									2006	1999	-8	2008			2013								
26	2005	2008	3	1991	2010	19							1999	1993	-6	2002	2010	8	2008								
25.5	1983	2004	21	1986	2004	18							1993	1988	-5	1997	2005	8	2002								
25		1992		1981	1997	16							1986	1981	-5	1992	1999	7	1997	2006	8						
24.5		1981		1976	1991	14							1979			1987	1993	6	1993	1996	3						
24					1985											1983	1987	4	1989	1991	1						
23.5					1980			2012			2007					1979	1981	2	1985	1986	1				2008		
23					1976		2008	2008	-1		1997					1975	1976	1	1981	1981	0				2003		
22.5							2002	2004	2		1989					1977	1977	0	1977	1977	0				1997		
22							1994	1997	3	1985	1980	-5													1991	2009	17
21.5							1986	1989	4													2009			1986	2000	15
21							1977	1981	4													2002	2004	2	1980	1990	10
20.5																						1996	1996	0	1975	1982	7
20																						1989	1988	-1			
19.5																						1984	1982	-1			
19																						1978	1977	-1			

Legend: Females — Males — S-time-distance (+): Male mean BMI behind female mean BMI (years) — S-time-distance (-): Male mean BMI ahead of female mean BMI (years)

FIGURE 15 S-time-distance view of regions comparing female and male levels of mean BMI for the period 1975 - 2014

SOURCE: Own calculations based on data from NCD-RisC (2016c).

Calculating these times by interpolations may pose a small problem of the degree of accuracy compared to the original data, but it offers additional understanding about the time dimension of disparities and a good summary overview. The result is a LEVEL-TIME MATRIX, which is easily understood by everybody.

The level-time matrix in Figure 15 is analyzing the regional data for the whole period 1975 – 2014. In the left column are mean value of BMI, in the body of the table in the first two columns are years in which these levels were attained, in the third column is the value of S-time-distance for the given level of the indicator. Such level-time matrix enables comparisons not only between males and females but also between countries and a visual impression of through how many steps of the indicator mean BMI a given region has evolved. Mean BMI for females was at the highest level for Central Asia, Middle East and North Africa, for males the highest level was in High-income Western countries.

The level-time matrix for selected countries in Figure 14 makes these visual comparisons even more apparent. Obviously the highest values for females are those in Egypt; while for the level of mean BMI 28.5 we can also calculate the S-time-distances between countries for females. The time lead of Egypt at this level was 16 years against USA, 17 years against Turkey, and 11 years against South Africa.

An interesting visual observation is that the gender difference in mean BMI for South Africa is so wide that in the four decades of available data there was no point of intersection, which means that the time lag for males must be over 40 years. This is an example when in the table of S-time-distances for mean BMI and obesity prevalence below the approximate indication of time distances more than 40 years or less than -40 years are presented.

Gender differences in obesity in a broader perspective: static and time distance dimensions

The next indicator from the selected indicators with the strong female – male distinctive characteristic is obesity. We have seen that, with the exception of two countries, life expectancy at birth is in favour of women. There are only 24 countries, for which men are ahead of women for obesity, mostly from High Income Western region. Also, none of them is ahead more than 20 years.

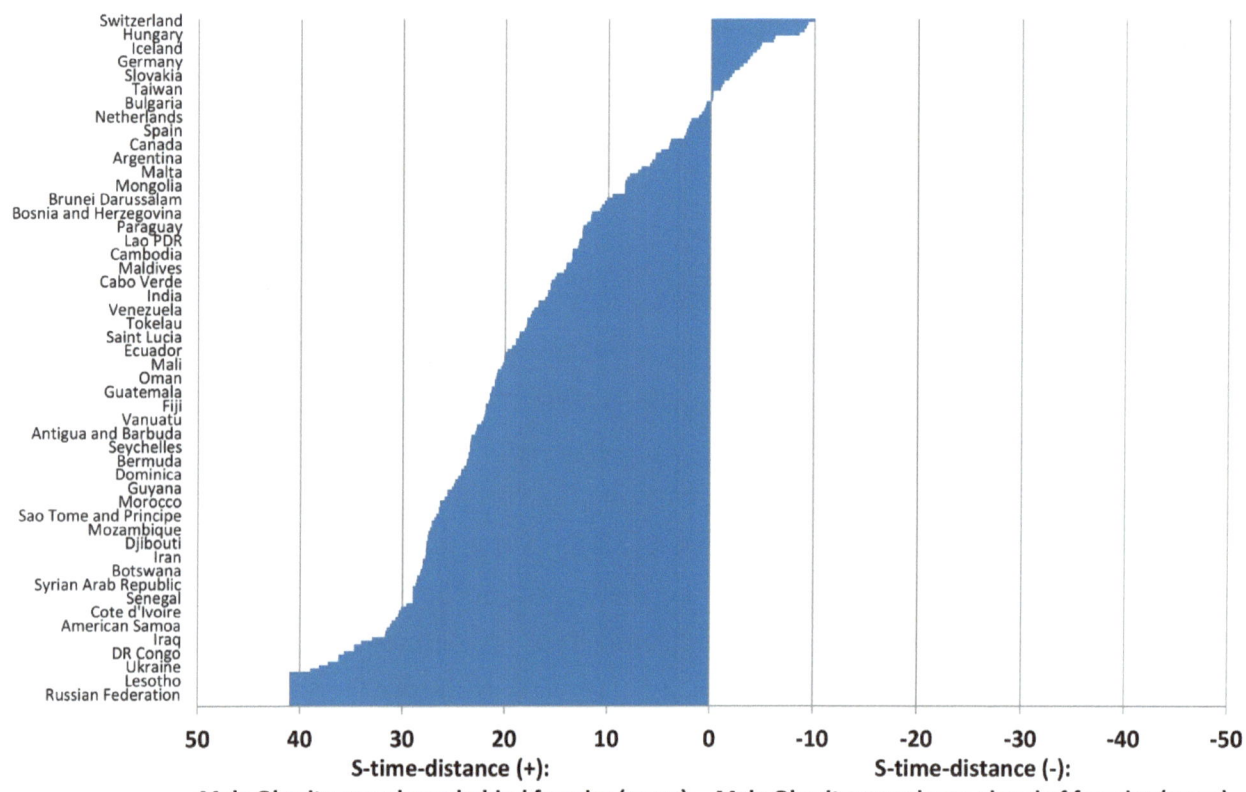

FIGURE 16 Comparing female and male levels of obesity in 2014
SOURCE: Own calculations based on data from NCD-RisC (2016c).

Table 17 shows for the world average shows time distance of about 14 years of women being ahead of men indicates that there are very large differences between countries in obesity prevalence. China and India show obesity prevalence below 10 percent, while for Egypt, Turkey and South Africa the female obesity percentages are at or above 36 percent. For United States of America the percentage is also high at 34 percent, for United Kingdom at 28 percent.

However, there is an important distinction in the time distance measure of male female difference in these countries, For United States of America and for the United Kingdom the obesity prevalence is high also for men so that gender time distances are only few years.

Obesity (%)	World Females	World Males	World S-time-distance	USA Females	USA Males	USA S-time-distance	UK Females	UK Males	UK S-time-distance	China Females	China Males	China S-time-distance	India Females	India Males	India S-time-distance	Egypt Females	Egypt Males	Egypt S-time-distance	Turkey Females	Turkey Males	Turkey S-time-distance	South Africa Females	South Africa Males	South Africa S-time-distance
39																2013								
38																2012						2014		
37																2010						2012		
36																2009			2014			2010		
35																2007			2012			2009		
34				2012												2006			2010			2007		
33				2010	2013	3										2005			2008			2006		
32				2008	2012	3										2003			2007			2004		
31				2006	2010	4										2001			2005			2002		
30				2005	2009	4										2000			2004			2001		
29				2003	2007	4										1999			2002			1999		
28				2001	2006	4	2013									1997			2000			1997		
27				2000	2004	5	2011									1995			1998			1995		
26				1998	2003	5	2010	2014	4							1994			1997			1993		
25				1997	2002	5	2008	2012	5							1992			1995			1991		
24				1995	2000	5	2006	2011	5							1990			1993			1989		
23				1994	1999	5	2004	2009	5							1989			1991			1986		
22				1992	1998	6	2003	2008	5							1987			1990	2014	24	1984		
21				1990	1996	6	2001	2006	5							1985	2014	28	1988	2012	23	1982		
20				1989	1995	6	2000	2005	5							1984	2012	28	1987	2010	23	1979		
19				1987	1993	6	1998	2003	5							1982	2010	28	1986	2008	23	1977		
18				1985	1992	7	1996	2002	5							1980	2009	28	1984	2006	22			
17				1983	1990	7	1994	2000	6							1979	2007	28	1982	2004	22			
16				1981	1988	7	1992	1998	6							1977	2005	28	1980	2002	22			
15				1979	1986	8	1990	1996	6							1975	2003	28	1978	2000	22			
14	2011			1977	1984	8	1988	1994	6								2001		1976	1998	22		2013	
13	2008				1982		1986	1992	6								1998			1996			2012	
12	2005				1979		1983	1989	5								1996			1994			2010	
11	2002				1976		1980	1986	5								1993			1991			2008	
10	1998	2012	14				1977	1982	4								1990			1989			2006	
9	1992	2009	16					1977									1987			1987			2004	
8	1986	2006	19							2013							1984			1985			2002	
7	1980	2002	22							2011	2013	3					1981			1982			1998	
6		1997								2008	2011	3					1977			1978			1995	
5		1990								2005	2009	4	2014										1990	
4		1983								2002	2007	5	2009										1984	
3										1997	2004	6	2004										1977	
2										1991	1999	8	1996	2012	16									
1										1980	1992	12	1984	2001	16									

Legend: Females (green) — Males (yellow)

S-time-distance (+): Male obesity behind female obesity (years)

FIGURE 17 S-time-distance view of selected countries comparing female and male levels of obesity prevalence for the period 1975 - 2014
SOURCE: Own calculations based on data from NCD-RisC (2016c).

For Egypt, Turkey and South Africa the time distances show large time differences of 28, 24 and more than 40 years, respectively. The example of South Africa shows that the two male and female values have never reached the same value in the 40 years range of data; the male value for 2013 was still lower than the lowest value for women in 1977.

Table 18 confirms the distinction on the regional level. High obesity prevalence for women in the region of High Income Western Countries are as high as in Oceania and Latin America and Caribbean, but the female male time distance is only 2 years as the obesity prevalence is also high for men. On the other hand, female obesity prevalence for Sub-Saharan Africa is distinctly lower than in the mentioned regions but the time distance of 31 years show a large time dimension of female male difference. The highest values of female obesity prevalence are in the Central Asia, Middle East and Northern Africa, with time distance of 24 years indicating high gender difference with women obesity being ahead of obesity prevalence over long time.

Obesity (%)	Central and Eastern Europe			Central Asia, Middle East and North Africa			East and South East Asia			High-income Asia Pacific			High-income Western countries			Latin America and Caribbean			Oceania			South Asia			Sub-Saharan Africa		
	Females	Males	S-time-distance	Females	Males	S-time-distance	Females	Males	S-time-distance	Females	Males	S-time-distance	Females	Males	S-time-distance	Females	Males	S-time-distance	Females	Males	S-time-distance	Females	Males	S-time-distance	Females	Males	S-time-distance
31				2013																							
30				2011																							
29				2010																							
28				2008																							
27				2006									2012	2014	2	2014			2014								
26				2005									2010	2012	2	2012			2012								
25				2003									2008	2010	3	2010			2010								
24				2001									2005	2008	3	2008			2008								
23	2010			1999									2003	2007	3	2006			2006								
22	2005			1997									2001	2005	4	2004			2003								
21	2001			1995									2000	2003	4	2002			2000								
20	1985	2014	29	1993									1998	2002	4	2000			1997								
19	1980	2012	32	1990	2014	24							1996	2000	4	1998	2014	16	1995								
18	1976	2010	34	1988	2012	24							1994	1998	5	1996	2012	17	1993								
17		2008		1986	2010	25							1991	1997	5	1993	2010	17	1991	2013	23						
16		2006		1983	2008	25							1989	1995	5	1991	2008	18	1988	2011	23						
15		2005		1981	2006	25							1987	1993	6	1988	2006	18	1984	2008	24						
14		2002		1979	2004	26							1985	1991	6	1986	2004	19	1981	2004	23						
13		2000		1976	2002	26							1982	1988	7	1983	2001	19	1978	2000	22				2013		
12		1994			1999								1979	1986	7	1980	1999	19		1996					2011		
11		1989			1996								1976	1983	7	1977	1996	19		1993					2008		
10		1986			1993									1980			1993			1989					2006		
9		1983			1989									1977			1990			1985					2004		
8		1979			1986		2014										1986			1980					2001		
7		1976			1983		2011										1982								1997		
6					1979		2008	2013	5								1979								1994		
5							2005	2011	5										2012						1989		
4							2002	2008	6		2014								2008						1982	2013	31
3							1997	2005	8	2005	2008	4							2002							2008	
2							1990	2000	10	1989	2000	11										1995	2011	16		2000	
1							1979	1992	13		1988											1983	1999	17		1983	

Legend: Females   Males   S-time-distance (+): Male obesity behind female obesity (years)

FIGURE 18 S-time-distance view of regions comparing female and male levels of obesity prevalence for the period 1975 - 2014
SOURCE: Own calculations based on data from NCD-RisC (2016c).

This is seen at a glance in Figure 19 showing S-time-distance view of regions comparing female and male levels of obesity prevalence for 2014. In one region High Income Asia Pacific the average value of obesity prevalence was in 2014 even higher than the obesity prevalence for women. As we see in Figure 18 the level of obesity in this region is very low for both sexes. Low time distance between sexes is also shown for High Income Western region and for East and South-East Asia.

There are four regions with time distances of more than 20 years indicating longer time prevailing higher levels of obesity prevalence for women than men: Sub-Saharan Africa with time distance higher than 30 years, followed by Central and Eastern Europe with time distance close to 30 years, Central Asia, Middle East and North Africa, and Oceania.

This confirms that gender differences in obesity prevalence are strongly tilted in the female predominance.

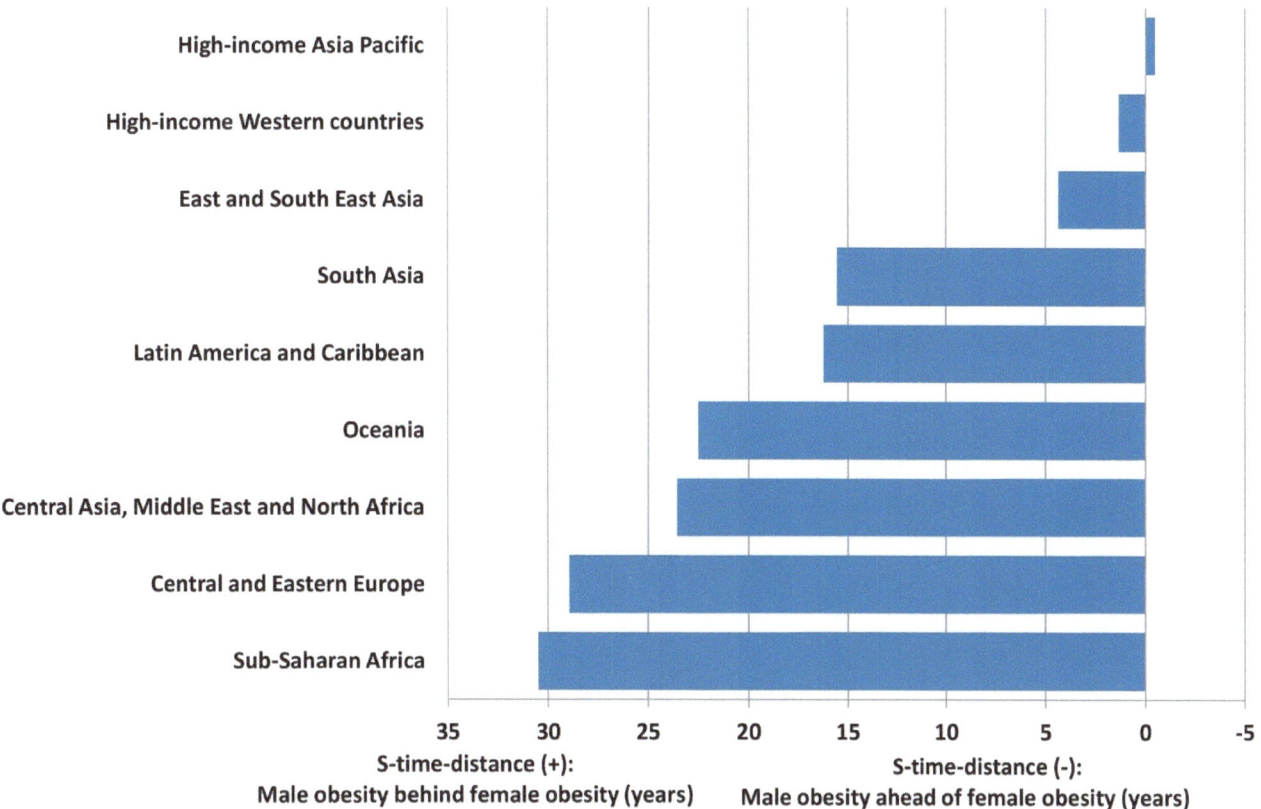

FIGURE 19 S-time-distance view of regions comparing female and male levels of obesity prevalence for 2014
SOURCE: Own calculations based on data from NCD-RisC (2016c).

Gender differences in diabetes in a broader perspective: static and time distance dimensions

Diabetes situation is a certain diversion from the three indicators that were studied until now in the sense that here one can see the predominance of cases for men in two high income regions, High Income Asia Pacific and in High Income Western countries. For diabetes the time series in the source NCD-RisC (2016c) are available for 35 years, i.e. for S-time-distance the value in Figure 20 as well as in the summary Table 6 can be reached only up to 35 years.

Another difference with respect to life expectancy or BMI indicator are the high percentage differences between sexes for diabetes. For life expectancy and BMI the percentage sex differences are much smaller. For instance, for BMI the perception based on percentage differences in 2014 (M/F) is moderate, from 11.8% higher for males in Switzerland to -16.7% for Swaziland, while the time distances indicate larger magnitude of sex differences in the time dimension. For diabetes the absolute range of diabetes prevalence indicators is much smaller so that percentage differences become much higher because of the small benchmark value.

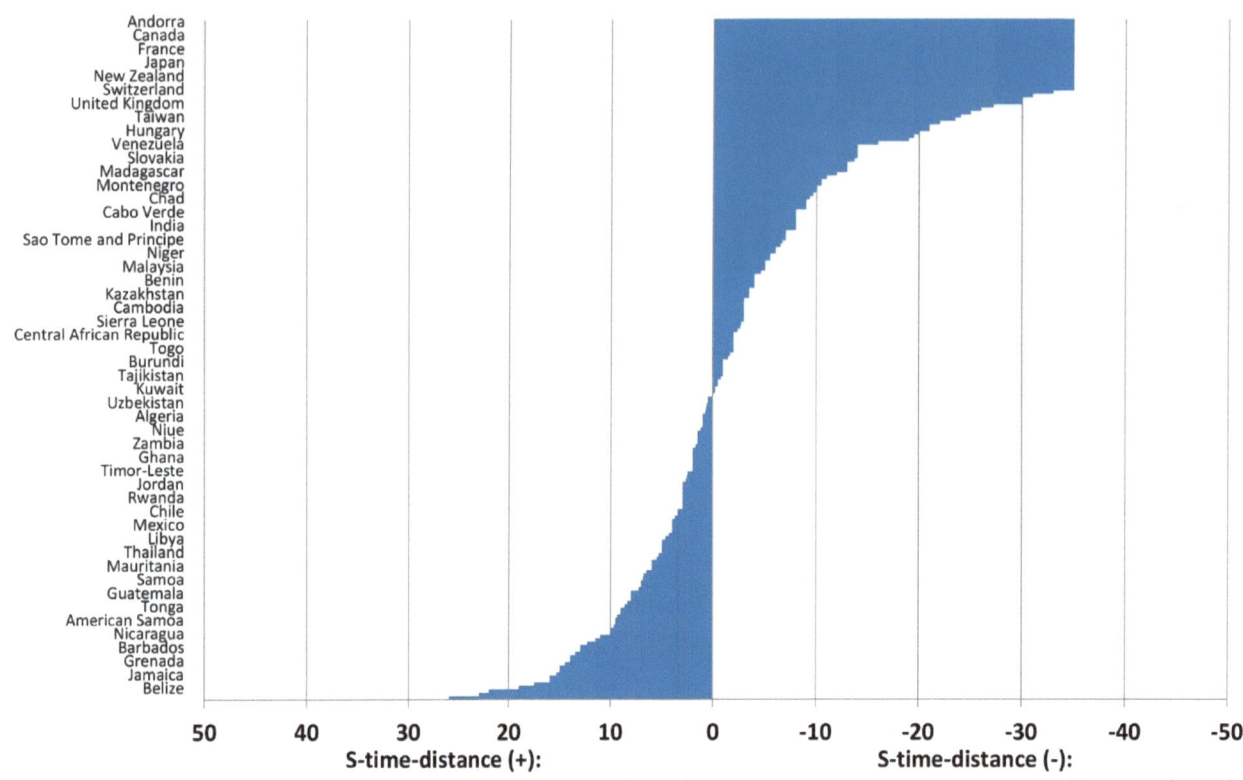

FIGURE 20 Comparing female and male levels of diabetes in 2014
SOURCE: Own calculations based on data from NCD-RisC (2016c).

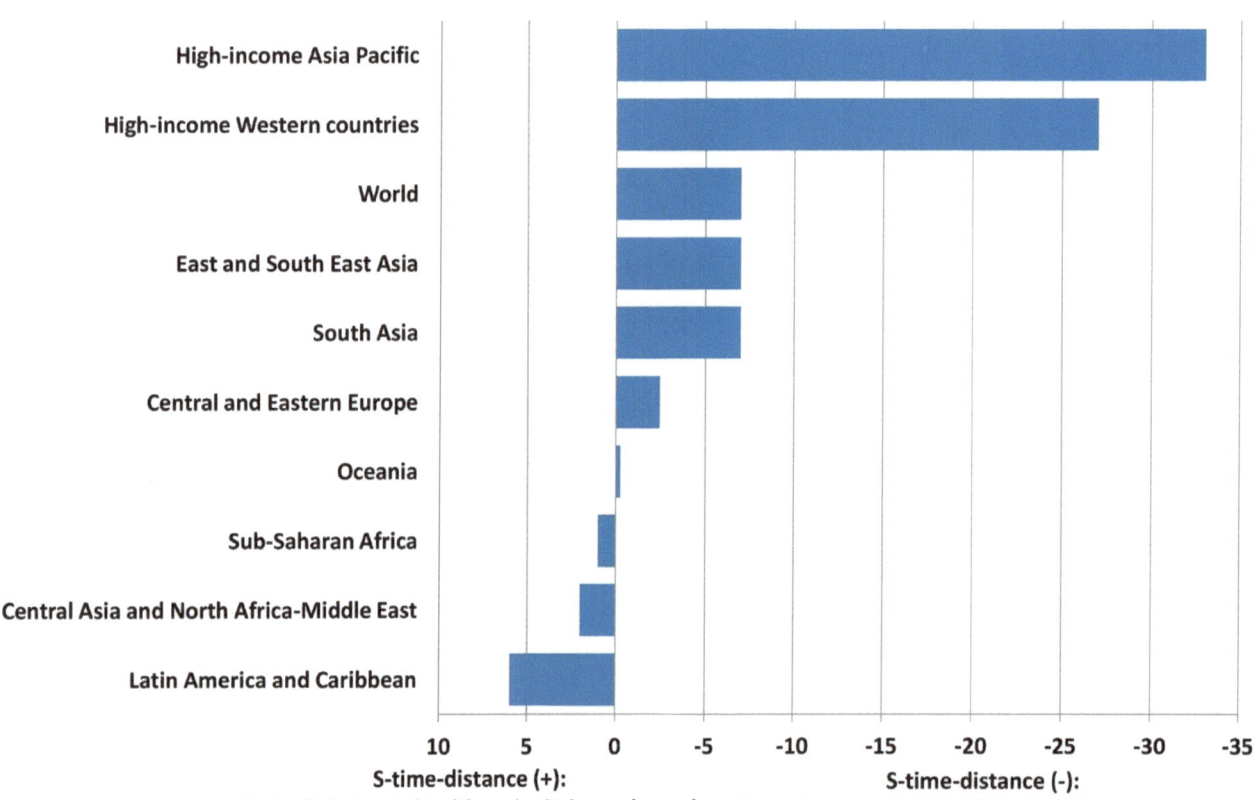

FIGURE 21 S-time-distance view of regions for sex differences of diabetes prevalence for 2014
SOURCE: Own calculations based on data from NCD-RisC (2016c).

There are 21 countries with male diabetes prevalence ahead of females for 35 years or more, and another 23 countries with time distances over 20 years. For the first group it means that in these countries the male prevalence rate was in the last 35 years always higher than for females indicating a long-term divergence and stability over time in the relative predominance of men over women for diabetes. On the other extreme, with female diabetes prevalence dominating over that of men there were only 3 countries with time distances over 20 years.

In 130 countries the sex differences expressed in time distance fall into the range up to 10 years of difference in either direction (see table in the Statistical Annex). For these countries also percentage differences are more modest. Male predominance is concentrated in certain regions, it is not an overall experience as it is the female prevalence in life expectancy.

Underweight

For the category Underweight (BMI being lower than 18.5) it is difficult to clearly look at the sex differences in the same way as for the other categories.

Underweight (BMI<18.5) (%)	Central and Eastern Europe			Central Asia, Middle East and North Africa			East and South East Asia			High-income Asia Pacific			High-income Western countries			Latin America and Caribbean			Oceania			South Asia			Sub-Saharan Africa		
	Females	Males	S-time-distance	Females	Males	S-time-distance	Females	Males	S-time-distance	Females	Males	S-time-distance	Females	Males	S-time-distance	Females	Males	S-time-distance	Females	Males	S-time-distance	Females	Males	S-time-distance	Females	Males	S-time-distance
36																						1977					
35																						1981	1976	-6			
34																						1985	1980	-5			
33																						1989	1984	-4			
32																						1992	1989	-4			
31																						1996	1993	-3			
30																						1999	1997	-2			
29																						2002	2000	-2			
28																						2004	2002	-2			
27																						2007	2005	-2			
26																						2009	2008	-2			
25																						2012	2010	-1			
24																							2013				
23																											
22																											
21																											
20																											
19																											
18																										1978	
17							1977																			1989	
16							1982																			1999	
15							1986															1981			1981	2005	24
14							1991	1977	-14													1989			1989	2010	22
13							1995	1988	-7													1997					
12							1999	1994	-5													2005					
11							2003	1998	-5	1977												2011					
10							2007	2002	-5	1984	1975	-9															
9							2011	2005	-6	1994	1979	-14															
8								2008		1984									1978								
7				1978	1980	2		2012		1989						1976	1977	1	1983								
6				1984	1985	2				1995						1982	1982	0	1989								
5				1991	1993	2				2004						1989	1988	-1	1996								
4				2001	2001	0							1980			1998	1994	-4	2005								
3	1981	1975	-6	2011	2008	-3							1991			2008	2001	-7	1980								
2		1986											2012	1975	-37		2010		2008								
1		2010												1992													

| Legend: | Females | Males | S-time-distance (+): Male underweight behind female underweight (years) | S-time-distance (-): Male underweight ahead of female underweight (years) |

FIGURE 22 S-time-distance view of regions comparing female and male levels of underweight prevalence for the period 1975 - 2014

SOURCE: Own calculations based on data from NCD-RisC (2016c).

On the one hand, eliminating the underweight population is an important overall world poverty problem and the trend must be towards decreasing the underweight prevalence. Thus the look at values in Figure 22 should be read in decreasing direction indicated by the calendar years when the values were attained. By year 2014 only two regions had underweight values for either sex above 10, while five regions had values much lower at about 3. With such low absolute levels the precision of derived measures is not easy to evaluate.

The only two world regions with underweight prevalence values higher than 10 are South Asia and Sub-Saharan Africa. South Asia managed in the period 1975-2014 to decrease the underweight values from about 36 to about 25, with little male-female difference as the values for both sexes decreased simultaneously, which produced time distances of only of about 2 years in the latest part of the period.

Prev185 (%)	World			Bangladesh			India			Philippines			Ethiopia			Indonesia			China		
	Females	Males	S-time-distance	Females	Males	S-time-distance	Females	Males	S-time-distance	Females	Males	S-time-distance	Females	Males	S-time-distance	Females	Males	S-time-distance	Females	Males	S-time-distance
37				1977			1977														
36				1983			1981	1977	-4												
35				1989			1985	1981	-4												
34				1994			1988	1985	-3												
33				1998			1992	1989	-3												
32				2001			1996	1994	-2												
31				2004	1983	-20	1999	1997	-2												
30				2006	1991	-16	2002	2000	-1												
29				2008	1996	-13	2004	2003	-1												
28				2011	2000	-11	2007	2005	-1												
27				2013	2003	-10	2009	2008	-1												
26					2006		2012	2010	-1							1976					
25					2009		2014	2013	-1	1976						1980					
24					2012					1979						1984					
23										1982						1987	1981	-6			
22										1985				1981		1990	1991	1			
21										1988			1977	2004	27	1993	1996	4			
20										1991			1989			1996	2000	5			
19										1994	1977	-17	2003			1999	2004	5			
18										1998	1984	-14	2010			2001	2006	5			
17										2003	1993	-10				2004	2009	4			
16										2007	1998	-9				2007	2011	4			
15										2011	2002	-9				2010	2014	4			
14	1980										2007					2013					
13	1989	1985	-4								2011								1978		
12	1998	1996	-2																1983		
11	2005	2002	-3																1988		
10	2012	2007	-4																1994	1981	-13
9		2013																	1998	1992	-6
8																			2002	1996	-6
7																			2006	1999	-6
6																			2009	2002	-7
5																				2005	
4																				2008	
																				2012	

Legend: Females | Males | S-time-distance (+): Male underweight behind female underweight | S-time-distance (-): Male underweight ahead of female underweight

FIGURE 23 S-time-distance view of selected countries comparing female and male levels of underweight prevalence for the period 1975 - 2014
SOURCE: Own calculations based on data from NCD-RisC (2016c).

Sub-Saharan Africa is the second region with high underweight prevalence values, yet at lower interval of 19 to 11 values. As distinct from South Asia, here women decreased the underweight values more than men, so that in Sub-Saharan Africa there are several countries where the decrease in underweight prevalence was predominant for women than men.

Figure 23 shows development for a selected number of countries and for the world aggregate. The figures for the world show that the sex differences with time distance about four years are a minor dissimilarity against the large regional or country inequality as seen in both figures. India and Bangladesh have shown good success but there values for underweight share still stay above other countries analysed. China has reached values around 7 for women and 4 for men, better than the world average.

Chapter 5

DUAL PARALLEL GENERIC SYSTEM FOR ANALYSING INDICATORS: ARE GENDER DIFFERENCES LARGE OR SMALL?

As mentioned in the Foreword, sustainable development is by definition a long-run and multi-dimensional phenomenon. Semantics of discussing the issues should not be based only on static measures; it needs to be complemented by dynamic measures. In Chapter 2 on time distance methodology it was explained that the present state-of-the-art does not realise that, in addition to static comparison, there exists in principle a theoretically equally universal measure of difference (distance) in time when a given level of the variable is attained by the two compared time series. It was shown that empirically the degree of disparity may be very different in static terms and in time distance. We need both, the static measure(s) and the time distance, to describe, perceive and evaluate the broader notion of gender differences in the concrete circumstances.

In the example of life expectancy for EU28 averages in Figure 1 it was shown that perceptions of the size of this gap can be very different depending on the statistical measure used. The static difference between two lines in 2015 was less than 7 percent (which may appear to be small if compared with gender differences in favour of men in many domains) while the S-time-distance was around 26 years (which gives a very different perception of the magnitude of the gap). In plain words, time distance measure tells the story that the male life expectancy value in 2015 was by females attained already 26 years ago, i.e. before 1990. Furthermore, it states that in the period of about of a quarter of a century there was no equalisation of gender life expectancy, i.e. that it was a long-lasting experience and that it does not seem to change easily.

When one compares the situation over more indicators or domains the comparisons of absolute differences in a given indicator (important in analysing particular field) face a very difficult problem of aggregating across different fields. Comparing over more indicators or domains is then usually done by static measures like percentages, indices or ratios. Such comparisons solve one problem but the face the problem of combining desired positive or negative tendencies (like positive life expectancy and negative direction for infant mortality). S-time-distance is invariant to monotonic transformations but requires relatively long time series if the relationships are prevailing over considerable period.

	S-time-distance (years)	Number of countries			
		Life expectancy (years)	Obesity (prevalence)	Mean BMI (kg/m2)	Diabetes (prevalence)
(-): Male ahead of female (years)	less than -40			2	21
	from -40 to -30			3	4
	from -30 to -20			15	9
	from -20 to -10		1	21	17
	from -10 to 0	2	23	20	60
(+) Male behind female (years)	from 0 to 10	55	28	34	70
	from 10 to 20	44	45	60	16
	from 20 to 30	52	74	28	3
	from 30 to 40	23	19	10	
	more than 40	24	10	7	
	Male ahead of female <0	2	24	61	111
	Female ahead of male >0	198	176	139	89
	All	200	200	200	200

TABLE 7 Summary of country results for 4 indicators over regions in 2014 and 2015
SOURCE: Own calculations based on data from NCD-RisC (2016c) and UN (2015).

Table 7 summarises results for S-time-distances over the four discussed indicators in Chapters 2 and 4, the frequency distribution across countries within the regions are provided in Statistical Annex.

It is easy to observe that the number of countries where the stability of male female relationship would prevail over many years in one or the other direction is very different for the four selected indicators. For the first three indicators the number of cases where the values for women are higher than for men are clearly prevailing, while for diabetes the countries with higher values for men are somewhat higher.

It is interesting to observe that in all four cases there is a number of countries in the order of 50 cases (for diabetes even 130 countries) where time distances between gender are not larger than 10 years in either direction. While one should look also at the magnitude of static differences (absolute or relative) the time distance values indicate that these are the cases where such gender differences are not constantly prevailing over a longer period of time. For life expectancy and obesity about half of the countries fall in a broader interval of time distances not being higher than 20 years; for mean BMI this number is even higher, for diabetes more than 160 countries fall in this range.

We arbitrarily set a time lead or time lag of gender difference to those time distances beyond duration of 20 years as indicating long persistent domination in time of a particular gender. For life expectancy and obesity about 100 countries fall into this category, in both fields the prevailing dominance is that of women with values being higher than that of men for more than at least for two decades. For life expectancy 24 countries showed time lead for women over 40 years.

For mean BMI and diabetes the outliers beyond time distances over 20 years can be found both for men and women. For mean BMI still higher number of countries with such large time distances for women (45 countries against 20 for men), while for diabetes the more numerous cases are those for men (34 countries with higher values for men against 3 countries in the other direction).

The distribution of countries by the value of S-time-distance measure for nine world regions (as defined by the NCD Risk Factor Collaboration) are presented in the Statistical Annex. For life expectancy the regions with time distances of male behind female higher than 20 years are Central and Eastern Europe, Latin America and Caribbean, High Income Western countries, following by Central Asia, Middle East and North Africa. Further regional details are available in Chapters 2 and 3. For obesity it is interesting that the highest number of countries of having time distances of male behind women of more than 20 years is Sub-Saharan Africa, followed by three other regions: Latin America and Caribbean, Central Asia, Middle East and North Africa, and Oceania.

For mean BMI now we have also regions with male ahead of females with time distances more than 20 years in 11 countries in High Income Western region and 5 countries in Central and Eastern Europe, while the opposite extremes are found in Central Asia, Middle East and North Africa, Sub-Saharan Africa, Oceania, and Latin America and Caribbean. For Diabetes it was shown that for 26 countries (out of 27 countries) in the region High Income Western Countries the male values were for more than 20 years ahead of those for women. This was the most outstanding feature of time distance calculations for diabetes gender differences.

Chapter 6

CONCLUSIONS

1. This study offers new insights by examining gender differences in life expectancy, mean body mass index, obesity and diabetes by using the novel time distance methodology. It combines two developments: firstly, recent availability of gender disaggregated longer time series by NCD Risk Factor Collaboration, 2016 on trends in body mass index in 200 countries over 40 years and on trends in diabetes in 200 countries over 35 years complemented the UN long time series on life expectancy over about 60 years. Secondly, such longer time series make possible productive application of S-time-distance methodology for describing and analyzing differences between females and males in the parallel dimension of time. As the focus in utilizing the available datasets we selected the gender difference in these indicators which can be attractive from both the medical and social standpoint and these results can be further elaborated in much more details with additional studies.

2. The conclusion that the gender disparity in life expectancy is very persuasive and a longstanding phenomenon is further confirmed by introducing the time distance statistical measure as another complementary perception of the degree of the female-male disparity in life expectancy. In graphical terms, the usual way to compare time-series is to look at the vertical dimension, i.e. for a given point in time. The S-time-distance approach provides an additional perspective, comparing time-series in the horizontal dimension, i.e. for a given level of the variable it looks at the difference in time when the compared units reached the same selected level of the indicator.

3. Empirically, the degree of disparity may be very different in static terms and in time distance, which leads to new conclusions and semantics important for policy considerations. This innovation opens the possibility for simultaneous two-dimensional comparisons of time series data in two specified dimensions: vertically (standard measures of static difference) as well as horizontally (Sicherl time distance), providing a new dimension of analysis to a variety of problems. They can give different perceptions of the order of magnitude of inequality within and between countries, as both dimensions matter. The time distance methodology is explained in Chapter 2 with further sources in the Appendix.

4. Such a broader concept of the overall degree of disparity can lead to a different perception of the extent of disparity than the conventional static measures alone. Comparing disparity in the overall life expectancy for the countries between China and Sweden the static difference against Sweden was in 2014 about 8 percent for China (which may appear to be small) and the S-time-distance was 34 years (which gives a very different perception of the magnitude of the gap). The approach is universal, understandable, and applicable to a wide variety of fields at both the macro and micro levels. Since time distance view provides an additional dimension of temporal disparity, results by other methods are left unchanged but new conclusions can be reached.

5. Chapter 2 reports on two issues. On the one hand it deals with the methodology of the time distance measure as additional perspective in measuring inequalities, the additional sources of the methodology are available in the Annex. There is a brief definition of two novel statistical measures: S-time-distance and S-time-step, followed by schematic presentation of conventional table format and additional complementary presentation in time distance approach. For visual presentation of levels the conventional table-format for time-series data is transformed into time matrix, which has a table-graph format and can be done over many units and many years. The identifiers in level-time matrix are units and selected levels of indicator while the corresponding times are in the main body of the table like Figure 2.

6. These methodological tools are then applied to analysis of sex differences in life expectancy, which show astonishing differences between countries. It is well known that, with exception of 2 countries, all around the world life expectancy at birth for women is higher than for men. The novel time distance methodology establishes that time series can be compared in two dimensions: 1. static gap for a given point in time in most conventional analysis, and 2. gap in time for a given level of the variable. Time distance is a notion that is applied in many fields, but S-time-distance is a special family of time distances that is defined for the same level of the indicator in the compared units. In the gender difference case for life expectancy one can address the question 'How many years ago did the current level of the male value reach the same level in the past trend for women?'. In Figure 1 time distance measure tells the story that for the EU averages the male life expectancy value in 2015 was by females attained already 26 years ago, i.e. before 1990; it was a long-lasting experience and that it does not seem to change easily.

7. With the broader view in two dimensions and the available longer time series data we can now describe the gender differences in many indicators simultaneously in static and time distance dimensions. It was established empirically the degree of disparity may be very different in static terms and in time distance. For life expectancy the time distance dimension of the diversion increases the perception of the degree of magnitude of sex difference in the indicator. In percentage terms in 2015 the range for 2000 countries varied from -2.9 percent in Swaziland to about 15 percent for Belarus. The perception of the magnitude of sex differences is very different as S-time-distances of women being ahead of men, varying from five year in favour of men in Swaziland to about 60 years! in Belarus. We need both measures to understand the reality.

8. Time lag for males behind females life expectancy for a given level of males on the world level is about 14 years, about 38 years for more developed regions in UN definition and about 11 years for the less developed regions. USA with 38 years and EU28 with 26 years are on one side and China with 12 years and India with 7 years on the other side. USA and EU28 are both showing very substantial and persuading differences in favour of women in these two developed regions, also at the regional NUTS levels in the EU and for the average of more than 3000 USA counties. The astonishing differences at the country level are established even at the static ranks, Table 4 shows nearly 20 countries where the rank of females of the country in the list of female life expectancy are for 22 to 58 places higher than the ranks of males in the corresponding male life expectancy. Another slightly shorter list of countries show the difference of 22 to 45 ranks in the other direction.

9. Chapter 3 analyses female-male disparity in life expectancy at birth for EU28 countries. With a smaller number of countries it is easier to analyse the topic in more detail and to elaborate the application of the time distance methodology. Therefore the methodological topics of time matrices, and the calculations of S-time-distances and S-time-steps for these countries are presented also in the novel visualisation format, showing the wealth of information in these tables. The astonishing differences in gender life expectancy between countries at the world level has been confirmed also for EU countries. Figure 9 presents a summary overview visualisation in the time matrix containing both female (F) and male (M) life expectances for EU countries in 56 rows for a period of around 65 years. The continuous block of 22 cases by highest life expectancy were females, only for six EU countries the female life expectancy was not higher than the male life expectancy in some above average EU countries.

The more detailed study of the EU countries has further strengthen the overall conclusion that the time distance method significantly indicated the large time distance perspective of the degree of disparity between female and male life expectancy that is not taken into account in the standard static analysis of disparities. Obviously, the application can be done for other regions or group of countries.

10. In Chapter 4 newly available longer time series of data allowed us extend the analysis of gender differences in life expectancy to three more indicators: mean body mass index, obesity, and diabetes. Here again there were many cases where the time lead or time lag of one gender were larger than 20 years, which was taken as indication that such gender differences prevailed over longer periods of time (in either direction).

The availability of 200 country data over the four decades in the NCD Risk Factor Collaboration study makes it possible to describe the magnitude of gender disparities in the time dimension in addition of the usual static or percentage differences. S-time-distance values range from more than 40 years of mean BMI values for males being ahead of mean BMI for females for Switzerland and Japan to more than 40 years of time lag in the opposite direction for 5 countries. This is a very different perception of the gender disparities in the countries as those of percentage differences at given point in time. The perception based on percentage differences in 2014 (M/F) is moderate, from 11.8% higher for males in Switzerland to -16.7% for Swaziland. This overall range of percentages does not give the impression that the gender difference would be very difficult to change over time.

An interesting visual observation in the time matrix is that the gender difference in mean BMI for South Africa is so wide that in the four decades of available data there was no point of being equal, which means that the time lag for males must be over 40 years. By regions the mean BMI for females was at the highest level for Central Asia, Middle East and North Africa, for males the highest level was in High-income Western countries.

11. Gender differences in obesity prevalence are strongly tilted in the female predominance. There are only 24 countries, for which men are ahead of women for obesity, mostly from High Income Western region. Also, none of them is ahead more than 20 years. China and India show obesity prevalence below 10 percent, while for Egypt, Turkey and South Africa the female obesity percentages are at or above 36 percent. For United States of America the percentage is also high at 34 percent, for United Kingdom at 28 percent.

However, there is an important distinction. For United States of America and for the United Kingdom the obesity prevalence is high also for men so that gender time distances are only few years. For Egypt, Turkey and South Africa the time distances show large time differences of 28, 24 and more than 40 years, respectively (for South Africa the male value for obesity in 2013 was still lower than the lowest value for women in 1977).

12. Diabetes situation is a certain diversion from the three indicators that were studied until now in the sense that here one can see the predominance of cases for men in two high income regions. Male predominance is concentrated in certain regions, it is not an overall experience as it is the female prevalence in life expectancy. For Diabetes it was shown that for 26 countries (out of 27 countries) in the region High Income Western Countries the male values were for more than 20 years ahead of those for women. This was the most outstanding feature of time distance calculations for diabetes gender differences.

13. For the category Underweight (BMI being lower than 18.5) eliminating the underweight population is an important overall world poverty problem and the trend must be towards decreasing the underweight prevalence. By year 2014 only two regions had underweight values for either sex above 10, while five regions had values much lower at about 3.

There are only two world regions with underweight prevalence values higher than 10: South Asia and Sub-Saharan Africa. South Asia managed in the period 1975-2014 to decrease the underweight values from about 36 to about 25, with little male-female difference as the values for both sexes decreased simultaneously, which produced time distances of only of about 2 years in the latest part of the period. Sub-Saharan Africa is the second region with high underweight prevalence values, yet at lower interval of 19 to 11 values. As distinct from South

Asia, here women decreased the underweight values more than men.

14. Chapter 5 summarises the results of the study as the dual parallel generic system for analysing indicators. Seeing with new eyes and providing new insights from existing data means deploying analytics in the parallel universe of time. Innovations: parallel additional generic statistical measures S-time-distance, S-time-step and Level-Time Matrix as presentation and visualization tool. Expressed in time units means that they are comparable across variables, fields of concern and units of comparison, which makes S-time-distance an excellent complementary analytical and presentation tool for policy and business debate offering additional insights, intuitive understanding, simplicity, and new semantics to many indicators and issues.

15. The methodology is applicable across many sectors and issues, both at macro and micro levels. In the information age this new parallel view of the existing databases is an important contribution to a more efficient utilization of the existing data. Time Matrix Calculator software will help the users to build time matrices from their own data for applications in numerous fields. In this study the immediate question was whether gender differences in life expectancy, mean BMI index, obesity and diabetes prevalence are large or small? In general it is expected that static and time distance measures of disparity can give different perceptions of the degree of inequality.

16. The availability of 200 country data over the four decades in the NCD Risk Factor Collaboration study makes it possible to describe the magnitude of gender disparities in the time dimension in addition of the usual static or percentage differences for the four selected indicators. From the rich material in these databases we selected to study gender differences as data were also disaggregated by sex. The empirical analysis strongly confirmed that different measures lead to different perceptions and that we need both types of measures (static difference and time distance) to understand the broader situations over time and units of comparison. We arbitrarily set a time lead or time lag of gender difference to those time distances beyond duration of 20 years as indicating long persistent domination in time of a particular gender. For life expectancy and obesity about 100 countries fall into this category, in both fields the prevailing dominance is that of women with values being higher than that of men for more than at least for two decades.

17. In the example of life expectancy for EU28 averages the static difference between two lines in 2015 was less than 7 percent (which may appear to be small if compared with gender differences in favour of men in many domains) while the S-time-distance was around 26 years (which gives a very different perception of the magnitude of the gap). Time distance measure tells a very different story that the male life expectancy value in 2015 was by females attained already 26 years ago, i.e. before 1990. In the period of about of a quarter of a century there was no equalisation of gender life expectancy, i.e. that it was a long-lasting and very persuasive experience.

18. It was observed that the number of countries where the stability of male female relationship would prevail over many years in one or the other direction is very different for the four selected indicators. For mean BMI and diabetes the outliers with time distances over 20 years can be found both for men and women. For mean BMI there was still higher number of countries with such large time distances for women (45 countries against 20 for men), while for diabetes the more numerous cases are those for men (34 countries with higher values for men against 3 countries in the other direction).

19. Region wise the details of S-time-distance values for nine world regions and the four indicators are presented in the Statistical Annex. It is interesting to observe that for all four indicators there is a number of countries in the order of 50 cases (for diabetes even 130 countries) where time distances between gender are not larger than 10 years in either direction. While one should look also at the magnitude of static differences (absolute or relative) the time distance values indicate that these are the cases where large gender differences are not constantly prevailing over a longer period of time.

20. In the study we concentrated on gender difference within countries in the four indicators, which can be of interest from both the medical and social standpoint for further studies. The availability of 200 country data over the four decades made it possible to describe the magnitude of gender disparities in two dimensions: static and time distance. It can be concluded that the time distance methodology can convey additional insights and understanding from the available data, in this and in other fields of concern. The gender disparity in life expectancy here is so much in favour of women around the globe in contrast to so many fields of concern where the gender disparity is in many countries very much tilted in the other direction. The comparisons of such fields would be expected.

21. This methodological and empirical results are useful input for more elaborated studies of the multiple factors behind the astonishing magnitude of country differences in the gender gap in life expectancy, mean BMI, obesity and diabetes that are very complex and interconnected; they include medical, social, and economic factors requiring large systematic research project(s).

REFERENCES

Eurostat (2012a), Life table, LIFEXP - Life expectancy at given exact age (ex).

Eurostat (2012b), Life expectancy at given exact age (ex) by NUTS 2 regions. Accessed July 6, 2012 (for females);accessed January 19, 2013 (for males).

Eurostat (2012c), Real adjusted gross disposable income of households per capita.

Granger C.W.J., Jeon Y. (1997), Measuring Lag Structure in Forecasting Models – The Introduction of Time Distance, Discussion Paper 97–24, University of California, San Diego.

Hausmann, R., Tyson, L.D., Zahidi, S. (2011), The Global Gender Gap Report 2011. World Economic Forum, Geneva, Switzerland.

Kulkarni et al. (2011), "Falling behind: life expectancy in US counties from 2000 to 2007 in an international context," Population Health Metrics 2011 9:16, doi:10.1186/1478-7954-9-16.

Monash University (2012), "It's in our genes: why women outlive men," http://www.monash.edu.au/news/show/3970. Accessed 5 August 2012.

NCD Risk Factor Collaboration (NCD-RisC) (2016a), Trends in adult body-mass index in 200 countries from 1975 to 2014: a pooled analysis of 1698 population-based measurement studies with 19•2 million participants, Lancet 2016; 387: 1377–96.

NCD Risk Factor Collaboration (NCD-RisC) (2016b), Worldwide trends in diabetes since 1980: a pooled analysis of 751 population-based studies with 4•4 million participants, Lancet 2016; 387: 1513–30.

NCD Risk Factor Collaboration (NCD-RisC) (2016c), Data downloads, http://www.ncdrisc.org/data-downloads.html. Accessed 22 April 2016.

Sicherl, P. (1973), "Time Distance as a Dynamic Measure of Disparities in Social and Economic Development," Kyklos XXVI(3): 559–575.

Sicherl, P. (1999), "A New View in Comparative Analysis", IB Revija, 1/1999, Ljubljana.

Sicherl, P. (2007), "The inter-temporal aspect of well-being and societal progress," Social Indicators Research 84: 231–247.

Sicherl, P. (2011), New Understanding and Insights from Time-Series Data Based on Two Generic Measures: S-Time-Distance and S-Time-Step. OECD Statistics Working Papers. 2011/09. OECD Publishing. Paris. http://dx.doi.org/10.1787/5kg1zpzzl1tg-en.

Sicherl, P. (2012), Time Distance in Economics and Statistics, New Insights from Existing Data, pp 444. Edition echoraum, Wien.

Sicherl, P. (2014a), Inter-Temporal Aspect of Wellbeing. In A. C. Michalos (Ed.), Encyclopedia of Quality of Life and Well-Being Research. Dordrecht, Netherlands: Springer, p. 3353-3363.

Sicherl, P. (2014b), How Much Longer Live Women Than Men Around the Globe? Astonishing Differences between Countries, Printed by CreateSpace, Charleston SC.

Sicherl, P. (2015), System for Monitoring Implementation of Targets: Present MDGs and Post-2015 SDGs, Printed by CreateSpace, Charleston SC.
http://www.gaptimer.eu/images/stories/System for Monitoring Implementation of Targets - Present MDGs and Post-2015 SDGs.pdf

UN (2011), Department of Economic and Social Affairs, Population Division, World Population Prospects: The 2010 Revision, CD-ROM Edition.

UN (2015), Department of Economic and Social Affairs, Population Division World Population Prospects: The 2015 Revision, DVD Edition.

UNDP (2007), United Nations Development Programme. "Women's political participation," Human Development Report 2007/2008, New York.

UNDP (2011), United Nations Development Programme. Human Development Report 2011, International Human Development Indicators, New York.

LIST OF FIGURES AND TABLES

Figures

Tables

APPENDIX

A1 Methodology

For methodology see freely available paper by Statistics Directorate, OECD:
P. Sicherl, New Understanding and Insights from Time-Series Data Based on Two Generic
Measures: S-time-distance and S-time-step; Working paper No. 44, Statistics Directorate, OECD
Publishing, Paris, November 2011.
Please download the paper on http://dx.doi.org/10.1787/5kg1zpzzl1tg-en.

More detailed methodological issues and numerous applications are available in the book:
Pavle Sicherl, Time Distance in Economics and Statistics, New Insights from Existing Data,
p. 444, Echoraum, Vienna, 2012.
More information is available on wikiprogress
http://www.wikiprogress.org/index.php/Time_Distance_in_Economics_and_Statistics

The book is available on amazon.de
http://www.amazon.de/gp/product/3901941274

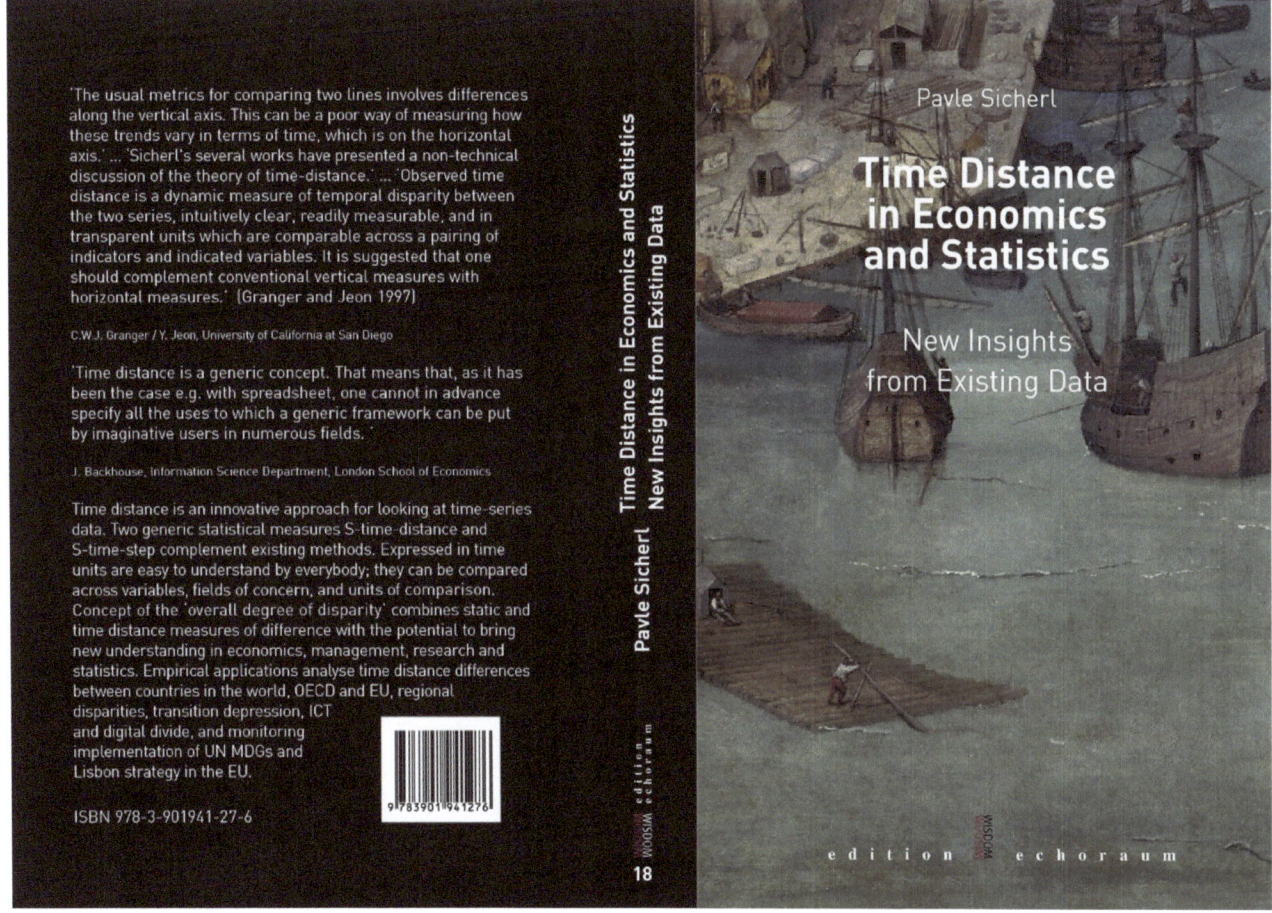

A2 Time Matrix Calculator to calculate time matrix for your own data

Example of input file
(for indicator life expectancy at birth)

Life expectancy at birth	1990	1991	1992	1993	1994	1995	1996	1997	1998	1999	2000	2001	2002	2003	2004	2005	2006	2007	2008	2009	2010	2011	2012
Belgium	76.2	76.3	76.5	76.5	76.8	77.0	77.3	77.5	77.6	77.7	77.9	78.1	78.2	78.3	79.0	79.1	79.5	79.9	79.8	80.1	80.3	80.7	80.5
Bulgaria	71.2	71.1	71.2	71.2	70.9	71.0	70.8	70.3	70.9	71.6	71.6	71.9	72.1	72.3	72.5	72.7	73.0	73.3	73.7	73.8	74.2	74.4	
Czech Republic	71.5	72.0	72.4	72.9	73.2	73.3	74.0	74.1	74.7	74.9	75.1	75.3	75.4	75.3	75.9	76.1	76.7	77.0	77.3	77.4	77.7	78.0	78.1
Denmark	74.9	75.3	75.3	75.2	75.5	75.3	75.7	76.1	76.5	76.6	76.9	77.0	77.1	77.4	77.8	78.3	78.4	78.4	78.8	79.0	79.3	79.9	80.2
Germany	75.4	75.7	76.2	76.2	76.6	76.7	77.0	77.4	77.8	78.0	78.3	78.6	78.6	78.6	79.3	79.4	79.9	80.1	80.2	80.3	80.5	80.8	81.0
Estonia	69.9	69.8	69.1	68.1	66.6	67.7	69.9	70.1	69.7	70.6	71.1	70.9	71.4	71.9	72.4	73.0	73.2	73.2	74.4	75.3	76.0	76.6	76.7
Ireland	74.8	75.0	75.4	75.3	75.8	75.5	75.8	76.0	76.2	76.1	76.6	77.2	77.7	78.2	78.6	79.0	79.3	79.7	80.2	80.4	80.6	80.8	80.7
Greece	77.1	77.1	77.0	77.4	77.5	77.5	77.6	77.9	77.9	77.9	78.2	78.8	79.0	79.1	79.3	79.5	79.8	79.7	80.2	80.4	80.6	80.8	80.7
Spain	77.0	77.1	77.6	77.7	78.1	78.1	78.2	78.7	78.8	78.8	79.3	79.8	80.3	80.3	81.1	81.1	81.5	81.9	82.4	82.6	82.5		
France	77.0	77.2	77.5	77.5	78.0	78.1	78.2	78.6	78.8	78.9	79.2	79.3	79.4	79.3	80.4	80.4	81.0	81.3	81.4	81.6	81.9	82.3	82.1
Croatia												74.6	74.7	74.6	75.4	75.3	75.9	75.8	76.0	76.3	76.7	77.2	77.3
Italy	77.1	77.1	77.5	77.8	78.0	78.3	78.7	79.0	79.1	79.6	79.9	80.3	80.4	80.1	80.9	80.9	81.4	81.6	81.7	81.8	82.2	82.4	82.4
Cyprus			77.2	77.1	77.4	77.7	77.4	77.2	78.0	77.7	79.0	78.7	79.0	79.1	78.7	80.1	79.8	80.6	81.0	81.5	81.2	81.1	
Latvia													70.2	70.6	70.9	70.6	70.6	70.8	72.1	72.8	73.1	73.9	74.1
Lithuania	71.5	70.6	70.5	69.0	68.6	69.1	70.3	71.1	71.4	71.8	72.1	71.6	71.8	72.0	72.0	71.2	71.0	70.7	71.7	72.9	73.3	73.7	74.1
Luxembourg	75.7	75.7	75.3	76.0	76.7	76.8	76.8	77.1	77.3	78.0	78.0	78.0	78.1	77.9	79.2	79.6	79.4	79.5	80.7	80.8	80.8	81.1	81.5
Hungary	69.4	69.4	69.2	69.2	69.6	70.0	70.6	71.1	71.0	71.1	71.9	72.5	72.6	72.6	73.0	73.0	73.5	73.6	74.2	74.4	74.7	75.1	75.3
Malta					77.2	77.3	77.6	77.5	77.4	78.4	78.9	78.8	78.7	79.4	79.4	79.5	79.9	79.7	80.4	81.5	80.9	80.9	
Netherlands	77.1	77.2	77.4	77.1	77.8	77.6	77.8	78.0	78.2	78.4	78.5	78.7	79.3	79.6	80.0	80.4	80.6	80.9	81.0	81.3	81.2		
Austria	75.8	75.9	76.1	76.3	76.7	76.9	77.1	77.5	77.9	78.1	78.3	78.8	78.8	79.0	79.5	80.1	80.4	80.6	80.5	80.8	81.2	81.1	
Poland	70.7	70.4	71.0	71.5	71.8	72.0	72.3	72.7	72.7	73.1	73.1	73.8	74.2	74.5	74.7	74.9	75.0	75.3	75.4	75.6	75.9	76.4	76.9
Portugal	74.1	74.1	74.7	74.6	75.5	75.4	75.3	75.8	76.0	76.2	76.8	77.2	77.4	77.5	78.4	78.2	79.0	79.3	79.5	79.7	80.1	80.7	80.6
Romania	69.9	70.1	69.5	69.5	69.4	69.3	68.8	69.1	69.9	70.6	71.2	71.1	71.0	71.4	71.9	72.3	72.8	73.3	73.5	73.6	73.8	74.6	74.5
Slovenia	73.9	73.8	73.7	73.6	74.0	74.7	75.2	75.2	75.3	75.7	76.2	76.4	76.6	76.4	77.2	77.5	78.3	78.4	79.1	79.4	79.8	80.1	80.3
Slovakia	71.1	71.1	71.5	72.0	72.5	72.4	72.9	72.9	72.8	73.2	73.3	73.6	73.8	73.8	74.2	74.1	74.5	74.6	74.9	75.3	75.6	76.1	76.3
Finland	75.1	75.5	75.7	75.9	76.7	76.7	77.0	77.2	77.4	77.6	77.8	78.2	78.3	78.6	79.0	79.1	79.5	79.6	79.9	80.1	81.3	81.5	81.8
Sweden	77.7	77.8	78.2	78.2	78.9	79.0	79.2	79.4	79.5	79.6	79.8	79.9	80.0	80.3	80.7	80.7	81.0	81.1	81.3	81.5	81.6	81.9	81.8
United Kingdom					76.2	76.8	76.7	77.0	77.2	77.4	77.5	78.0	78.2	78.3	78.4	79.0	79.2	79.7	79.9	80.2	80.6	81.0	81.0

Source: Eurostat (2013a), Life expectancy by age and sex, Total [demo_mlexpec].

Time matrix for life expectancy at birth

LEVEL	67	68	69	70	71	72	73	74	75	76	77	78	79	80	81	82
Spain											1990	1994	1999	2003	2006	**2009**
Italy												1994	1997	2000	2006	**2010**
France											1990	1994	1999	2004	2006	**2010**
Sweden												1992	1995	2002	**2006**	
Cyprus												2000	2005	2007	**2009**	
Netherlands												1999	2004	2006	**2010**	
Austria										1992	1996	1999	2003	2006	**2011**	
Luxembourg										1993	1997	2003	2004	2007	**2011**	
Malta												2000	2003	2008	**2011**	
United Kingdom												1996	1999	2004	2007	**2012**
Germany											1992	1996	1999	2004	2007	**2012**
Greece											1992	1999	2002	**2008**		
Ireland									1991	1997	2001	2003	2005	**2008**		
Finland									1993	1996	2001	2004	**2009**			
Belgium										1995	2001	2004	**2009**			
Portugal									1993	1998	2001	2004	2006	**2010**		
Slovenia								1994	1996	2000	2004	2006	2008	**2011**		
Denmark										1997	2001	2004	2009	**2011**		
Czech Republic					1991	1993	1996	2000	2005	2007	**2011**					
Croatia								2004	2008	**2011**						
Poland					1992	1995	1998	2001	2005	**2009**						
Estonia	1994	1995	1996	1998	2001	2003	2005	2008	2009	**2010**						
Slovakia						1993	1999	2004	2008	**2011**						
Hungary				1995	1998	2000	2005	2008	**2011**							
Romania			1997	1998	2002	2004	2006	**2010**								
Bulgaria					1998	2002	2007	**2011**								
Latvia					2007	2008	2010	**2012**								
Lithuania			1995	1996	2007	2008	2009	**2012**								

Available software tool:
Time Matrix Calculator

Faculty of Social Sciences, University of Ljubljana and SICENTER, Ljubljana, Slovenia

Methodology: Professor Pavle Sicherl
Programming: May Doušak
Testing: Jaka Hajnšek

www.timedistance.net

Required format of the input file:
Input file is an Excel file with data table in active sheet.
In the row 1 there are time units (number format) from cell B1 to the right; in the column A are unit names (text format, e.g., countries, regions, etc.) from cell A2 down.

Time matrix condenses information over many units and years (from about 550 entries in the input file), into much smaller number of about 140 entries, **which is a great advantage for presentation and visualisation providing a good summary overview of the situation at a glance**.

The year presented in **bold** show the latest presented year of the indicator for the given country. It can help to quickly observe whether there was a noticeable decrease in later years in the observed period.

STATISTICAL ANNEX

TABLE AN1 Results of S-time-distance gender comparisons over regions for life expectancy

Life expectancy (years) / S-time-distance (years)	Number of countries									
	All	Sub-Saharan Africa	Central Asia, Middle East and North Africa	South Asia	East and Southeast Asia	Oceania	High-income Asia Pacific	Latin America and Caribbean	High-income Western countries	Central and Eastern Europe
(-): Male ahead of female (years) — less than -40										
from -40 to -30										
from -30 to -20										
from -20 to -10										
from -10 to 0	2	2								
(+) Male behind female (years) — from 0 to 10	55	40	2	6	4			2		
from 10 to 20	44	4	14		4	6	2	5	6	1
from 20 to 30	52		5		3	2	1	12	16	4
from 30 to 40	23	1	2		4	1		9	3	2
more than 40	24	1	5					4		13
Male ahead of female <0	2	2	0	0	0	0	0	0	0	0
Female ahead of male >0	198	46	28	6	15	9	3	32	25	20
All	**200**	**48**	**28**	**6**	**15**	**9**	**3**	**32**	**25**	**20**

SOURCE: Own calculations based on data from UN (2015).

TABLE AN2 Results of S-time-distance gender comparisons over regions for obesity prevalence

Obesity (prevalence) / S-time-distance (years)	Number of countries									
	All	Sub-Saharan Africa	Central Asia, Middle East and North Africa	South Asia	East and Southeast Asia	Oceania	High-income Asia Pacific	Latin America and Caribbean	High-income Western countries	Central and Eastern Europe
(-): Male ahead of female (years) — less than -40										
from -40 to -30										
from -30 to -20										
from -20 to -10	1								1	
from -10 to 0	23				2		1		12	8
(+) Male behind female (years) — from 0 to 10	28		4		3		2	1	13	5
from 10 to 20	45	5	5	5	10	2		13	1	4
from 20 to 30	74	30	11	1		12		20		
from 30 to 40	19	10	4			2		1		2
more than 40	10	3	4		1	1				1
Male ahead of female <0	24	0	0	0	2	0	1	0	13	8
Female ahead of male >0	176	48	28	6	14	17	2	35	14	12
All	**200**	**48**	**28**	**6**	**16**	**17**	**3**	**35**	**27**	**20**

SOURCE: Own calculations based on data from NCD-RisC (2016c).

TABLE AN3 Results of S-time-distance gender comparisons over regions for mean BMI

Mean BMI (kg/m2)	S-time-distance (years)	All	Sub-Saharan Africa	Central Asia, Middle East and North Africa	South Asia	East and Southeast Asia	Oceania	High-income Asia Pacific	Latin America and Caribbean	High-income Western countries	Central and Eastern Europe
(-): Male ahead of female (years)	less than -40	2						1		1	
	from -40 to -30	3								2	1
	from -30 to -20	15				2		1		8	4
	from -20 to -10	21					1	1		10	9
	from -10 to 0	20	2	2	1	3			3	5	4
(+) Male behind female (years)	from 0 to 10	34	6	9	4	6	1		8		
	from 10 to 20	60	26	4	1	4	5		17	1	2
	from 20 to 30	28	6	9		1	6		6		
	from 30 to 40	10	3	2			4		1		
	more than 40	7	5	2							
	Male ahead of female <0	61	2	2	1	5	1	3	3	26	18
	Female ahead of male >0	139	46	26	5	11	16	0	32	1	2
	All	200	48	28	6	16	17	3	35	27	20

SOURCE: Own calculations based on data from NCD-RisC (2016c).

TABLE AN4 Results of S-time-distance gender comparisons over regions for diabetes prevalence

Diabetes (prevalence)	S-time-distance (years)	All	Sub-Saharan Africa	Central Asia, Middle East and North Africa	South Asia	East and Southeast Asia	Oceania	High-income Asia Pacific	Latin America and Caribbean	High-income Western countries	Central and Eastern Europe
(-): Male ahead of female (years)	less than -35	21				1		2		18	
	from -35 to -30	4								4	
	from -30 to -20	9				1	1	1		4	2
	from -20 to -10	17	4	1			2		1	1	8
	from -10 to 0	60	26	12	5	6	2		1		8
(+) Male behind female (years)	from 0 to 10	70	13	15	1	7	12		21		1
	from 10 to 20	16	5						10		1
	from 20 to 30	3				1			2		
	from 30 to 35										
	more than 35										
	Male ahead of female <0	111	30	13	5	8	5	3	2	27	18
	Female ahead of male >0	89	18	15	1	8	12	0	33	0	2
	All	200	48	28	6	16	17	3	35	27	20

SOURCE: Own calculations based on data from NCD-RisC (2016c).

ABOUT THE AUTHOR

Professor Pavle Sicherl, Founder of SICENTER and principal researcher, 1993-present, Professor of Economics, University of Ljubljana, Slovenia (1975-2003); macroeconomic adviser in the Harvard University Development Advisory Service team in Ethiopia, (1970-1974); in 1960's Deputy Director of the Yugoslav Institute of Economic Research in Belgrade.

Born in Ljubljana, Slovenian citizen. Ph.D. (economics) and Dipl.Econ., University of Ljubljana; M.A. Development Economics (Williams College, MA, USA). Speciality: growth and inequality, he introduced a new statistical measure, S-time-distance, to amend the present methods of analysing time-series data and disparities in many fields.

For this idea he received many fellowships and invitations: Senior Fulbright Research Award (Yale), London School of Economics, Institute of World Economics (Kiel), Institute for Advanced Studies (Vienna), etc. Visiting professor abroad, project leader for international and national projects, and consultant to the World Bank, OECD, UN, ILO, UNIDO, INSTRAW, ITU, EUROCHAMBRES.

Biography: Who's Who in the World, Marquis, 1991-1992 ... 2016, Who's Who in Science and Engineering, Marquis, 2016-2017.

Website: www.gaptimer.eu

Email: pavle.sicherl@gaptimer.eu

GAPTIMER REPORTS SERIES

In the Gaptimer Report Series there are three existing report that are useful background studies to the analysis of the MDGs and their monitoring of implementation, as well as important on their own position on development issues as Human Development Index, How much longer Live Women than Men around the World, and European Union at a Glance.

Brief information on these reports is provided here. The electronic versions of the reports are available on our web site www.gaptimer.eu. The printed copies of the reports are available on Amazon.com.

No. 1 World Inequalities in Human Development Index

Gaptimer Report No. 1 'World Inequalities in Human Development Index' presents a new way of understanding and discussing development and world inequalities in a new dynamic framework. Time distance methodology can be very helpful both in the preparation of the post-2015 agenda as well as in the continuous monitoring of implementation of selected indicators later, both on the aggregate and national levels. The first step in building any strategy is the assessment of the starting position. This report analyses it for the domain of the Human Development Index (HDI), it is applicable to indicators in other domains, including MDGs.

This manuscript can expand knowledge in two ways. Firstly, it offers an innovative approach for looking at disparities over many units and over time. The new time distance measure, expressed in time units, is easy to understand by everybody and offers a novel way to compare situations in economics, politics, business and statistics. The time distance concept can influence the perception and decisions of people when they are assessing their relative position in their surroundings, in the society and across countries over time.

The empirical results for the HDI over the three decades (1980-2012) provide new insights for the post-2015 agenda. S-time-distance measure (calculations based on official UNDP data) estimates HDI inequalities for each of 187 countries within their peer group. Telling new stories includes inequalities within EU27, BRICS countries, and Gulf Coordination Council countries.

Describing and perceiving inequalities in terms of percentages and ranks is not enough. Development processes take place in time and to get additional insights from existing data we complement the static measures of inequality by measuring the gap in time when two compared countries achieved the same level of the indicator (i.e., the HDI level of 0.55 was attained in China in 1996 and in India in 2011, showing S-time-distance lag of 15 years behind Sweden). For life expectancy the static difference for China against Sweden was less than 10 percent (which may appear to be small) while the time distance was around 50 years (which gives a very different perception of the magnitude of the gap, the life expectancy in China in 2012 was attained in Sweden in 1964).

No. 2 How Much Longer Live Women than Men Around the Globe?

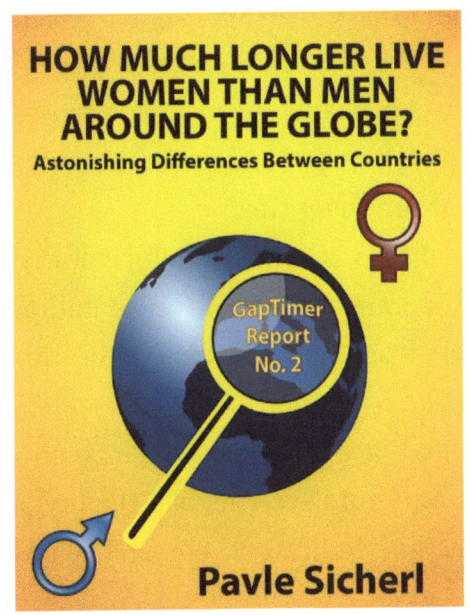

This report concentrates on gender disparity in life expectancy at various levels (at the world level for 196 countries and some aggregates; for EU27 countries with 269 NUTS2 regions, and draws conclusion also from the study of more than 3000 USA counties). The statistical results show the gender disparity in life expectancy is so much in favour of women thus standing out against so many domains where the gender disparity is in many countries leaning in the other direction. However, analysing this gender gap of life expectancy the main focus is on the striking differences between countries around the globe.

The book offers new insights by examining gender disparity in life expectancy by using the novel generic time distance methodology. Sustainable development is by definition a long-run and multi-dimensional phenomenon. Semantics of discussing the issues, in setting the targets and in the implementation should not be based only on static measures; it needs to be complemented by dynamic measures. This methodology presents an innovation that goes beyond the present state-of-the art in measuring the degree of inequality mainly on static relative measures thus increasing the understanding of the situation in the time perspective. The time distance methodology could be very useful for analysing indicators of gender disparity in many other domains.

The empirical results concentrate on gender disparity in life expectancy around the globe (at the world level for 196 countries and some aggregates; for EU27 countries with 269 NUTS2 regions). While female life expectancy at birth is higher than that for males for 99.5 percent of the world population, there are astonishing differences among countries. For example, Estonia occupied rank 51 the world for females and 110 for males. On the other extreme, e.g. the rank for Qatar was 65 for females and only 12 for males.

The time distance measure shows the reality with new eyes. The overall life expectancy the static difference between China and Sweden was less than 10 percent (which may appear to be small) while the S-time-distance was 51 years, (which gives a very different perception of the magnitude of the gap). For gender disparity in life expectancy S-time-distance for the world average, i.e. the horizontal time gap between trends of female and male life expectancy amounted to 20 years, 28 years for the EU27 and 35 years for the USA, showing a large and persistent gap in favour of women.

No. 3 European Union at a Glance

European Union at a Glance presents an easily understandable overview of 30 selected indicators over 28 EU countries in time, which is probably the most condensed current summary picture of disparities and dynamics in the EU countries over many domains over time.

It uses innovative time matrix presentation format that enables such condensed summary visual presentation. These 30 selected indicators from many Eurostat indicators systems follow the orientation of Beyond GDP.

Time matrices presented are based on rearranging Eurostat data for 30 selected indicators from many Eurostat indicators systems like Quality of life, Sustainable Development Indicators, Digital Agenda, Headline Indicators, etc. and follow the orientation of Beyond GDP.

The voyage through 30 time matrices for 28 countries compressed a very large amount of data, expressing multidimensional nature of development and well-being, indicating both visually and in numbers that very large differences exist between EU countries with respects to levels and dynamics of indicators. Using the innovative approach of time distance methodology the telling power of S-time-matrix format provided a good summary overview at-a-glance over many domains with clear understanding to decision-makers as well as to the general public. Seeing with new eyes creates new knowledge and better understanding.

Statistical offices of international organisations as well as national statistical offices, NGOs, experts and students could also use the time matrix presentation to complement their usual time series data tables covering many years and units. It can be used in publications, web pages and other software as a first-level visualisation tool to 'turn statistics into knowledge'.

No. 4 System for Monitoring Implementation of Targets - Present MDGs and Post-2015 SDGs

The study serves two purposes. The novel time distance methodology leads to the main part of empirical results dealing with monitoring implementation of the 10 selected MDG indicators over seven world regions, China, and India; and in details for five MDG indicators for 127-157 countries. This indicates that the method could be immediately applied for the post-2015 SDGs.

This methodology adds the possibility to look at indicator differences in the parallel universe of time, adding new vocabulary and not replacing the current methods. S-time-distance as a special category of time distances is defined for a given level of the variable. In application for monitoring implementation of targets (deviations from the line to target) it is like comparing train or air plane arrivals with the timetable provided. It is applicable to many domains and levels (world, national, regional, local, business, and various disaggregations). Together with software tool may contribute to internal discussion of results at national level for MDGs and other targets for many countries.

In the Gaptimer Progress Chart for four MDG indicators the 2015 targets were achieved in the majority of world regions; for three MDG indicators the target was not achieved in any of the world region, similarly not in any of the 10 selected indicators for the Sub-Saharan region.

The time distance view of discrepancy is even more pronounced at the level of countries. Long time lags behind the line to target for some can mean either poor performance or unrealistic MDG targets. This highlights the importance of better balance between desirability and feasibility in preparing SDG targets.